DAVID R ROSS is at his happiest stravaiging Scotland on his motor-cycle, rummelling around ruins and battle sites, and standing on the spots where the great and not so great Scots of history stood. Real happiness is when you are so engrossed in whatever you are doing that time has no meaning, and you forget to eat, till the rumbling in your stomach reminds you that it has been many hours since you last saw food.

He has tried to change his ways and become a gentleman motorcyclist, and to drive for the sake of driving, rather than driving to arrive.

During a recent court appearance, his lawyer, trying hard to convince the judge at some length of Mr Ross's integrity and that his excessive speed was a great misjudgement, held up copies of his books and announced that his client was indeed the 'biker historian'. The judge, face solemn, replied, 'I hope you are not going to read them out to me.'

Ross then sold his beloved Kawasaki ZZR 1100 for an emin-ently more sedate and sensible Honda Pan European but has since been shocked to find that it is not the motorcycle that has been at fault but a heavy right hand on the accelerator.

He loves Scotland, as will be obvious to all who have had the misfortune to listen to him rant on. He knows that it has many faults, but the way he sees 'his' Scotland will be apparent to any-one who turns these pages. He genuinely thinks he has been lucky, being born in a country with such a heritage and history. He is lucky that it is neither too big nor too small and that one lifetime is just sufficient to get to know it intimately. He wishes that he could have stood in the front line at Bannockburn, and although he is lucky to be Scottish, the timing was a bit out.

By the same author:
On the Trail of William Wallace (1999)
On the Trail of Robert the Bruce (1999)
On the Trail of Bonnie Prince Charlie (2000)

A Passion for Scotland

DAVID R. ROSS

Luath Press Limited

EDINBURGH

www.luath.co.uk

First published 2002

The paper used in this book is recyclable.
It is made from low chlorine pulps produced in a low energy,
low emission manner from renewable forests.

Printed and bound by
Bell & Bain Ltd, Glasgow

Typeset in Sabon

Contents

The sites of death and final resting places of the Kings of Scots

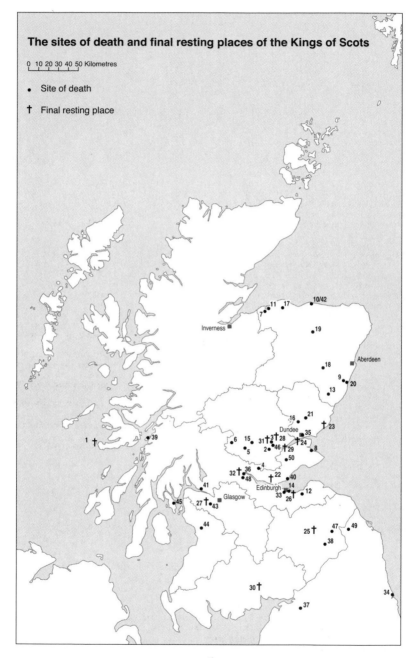

0 10 20 30 40 50 Kilometres

•   Site of death

†   Final resting place

Key

1 Iona.
2 Forteviot, where Kenneth MacAlpin died.
3 Mouth of the River Almond, where Donald MacAlpin was stabbed to death.
4 Dollar, where Constantine I was beaten in battle by the Vikings. One source says he was chased and slain at Inverdovat, which may be near Newport-on-Tay.
5 Blairinroar, where Aed was slain at the Battle of Strathallan.
6 Dundurn, near St. Fillans, where Giric was slain.
7 Forres, where Donald II died.
8 St. Andrews, where Constantine II died and was buried before his transferral to Iona.
9 Fetteresso, where Malcolm I died in battle.
10 Cullen, where King Indulf died in battle against the Vikings.
11 Kinloss, where Dubh's murdered body was found under a bridge.
12 Lothian, where Culen was slain.
13 Fettercairn, where Kenneth II was slain.
14 River Almond, where Constantine III was murdered.
15 Monzievaird, where father and son Kenneth III and Giric II both died in battle.
16 Glamis, where Malcolm II died of injuries received in battle.
17 Elgin, where Duncan died of wounds received in battle at nearby Pitgaveny.
18 Lumphanan, where Macbeth was slain.
19 Strathbogie, where Lulach was slain.
20 Stonehaven, where Duncan II was slain.
21 Forfar, where Donald III was murdered.
22 Dunfermline Abbey, last resting place of Malcolm Canmore and his queen St. Margaret (subsequently moved to Madrid), and all of their sons including King Edgar, Alexander I and his queen Sibylla, David I and his two queens, and Malcolm IV (The Maiden). After a gap, it also became the last resting place of Alexander III and his first queen, Robert the Bruce and his queen.
23 Arbroath Abbey, last resting place of William I (The Lion) who founded the abbey.
24 Balmerino Abbey, last resting place of Ermengarde, queen of William the Lion.
25 Melrose Abbey, last resting place of Alexander II.
26 Holyrood Abbey, last resting place of David II, James II, James V and his queen Magdalen, and Darnley, husband of Mary Queen of Scots. Mary of Gueldres, queen of James II, was transferred here after the demolition of Trinity College Church.
27 Paisley Abbey. Paisley is the last resting place of Bruce's daughter Marjory, her husband Walter and the two queens of Robert II are here. Robert III has a later tomb marking his internment here.
28 Scone Abbey: nothing remains of the original abbey, but Robert II is buried here.
29 Lindores Abbey: this ruin is the site of the burial place of David, Duke of Rothesay, son of Robert III, who was murdered although he was heir to the throne.
30 Lincluden College, Dumfries: Princess Margaret, sister of the aforementioned Prince David is buried here.
31 Carthusian monastery, Perth, last resting place of James I, his queen Joan, and also Margaret Tudor, queen of James IV.
32 Cambuskenneth Abbey, last resting place of James III and his queen Margaret of Denmark.
33 Edinburgh Castle, where St. Margaret died. David II also died here.
34 Tynemouth: Malcolm Canmore died here in battle.
35 Dundee: King Edgar died here.
36 Stirling: both King Alexander I and William the Lion died in the Castle.
37 Carlisle: King David I died on a visit here.
38 Jedburgh: King Malcolm IV, the Maiden, died here.
39 Kerrera: King Alexander II died on the island.
40 Kinghorn: King Alexander III died at nearby Pettycur Bay. A monument marks the spot.
41 Cardross: Robert the Bruce died at his manor here, north of Dumbarton. It is not to be confused with Cardross on the Clyde.
42 Cullen: Bruce's queen Elizabeth died here.
43 Paisley: Princess Marjorie Bruce died at Gallowhill in Paisley. A monument marks the spot. Her husband, Walter the Steward, died at Bathgate.
44 Dundonald Castle: Robert II died here.
45 Rothesay: Robert III died in the castle.
46 Perth: James I was murdered in the Blackfriars monastery.
47 Roxburgh Castle: James II was killed by an exploding cannon here.
48 Bannockburn: King James III was murdered at Beatons Mill after the Battle of Sauchieburn.
49 Flodden: King James IV died on the field of battle.
50 Falkland: King James V died in the Royal Palace.

Acknowledgements

THANKS TO ALL IN Canada who made my trip so special, especially Lynn Boland Richardson; to all of the Wallace Clan of North America; to Ross Hunter for his friendship and hard work; to Fiona Watson for her input and guidance; to Linda Donnelly for typing up the rough draft. Thanks to Donnell for scanning photos because I am too lazy to learn to work computers properly. To Daphne Thurlow – James IV would appreciate you!

Thanks to the Society of William Wallace, and to all those people, some mentioned in these pages, whom I meet wherever I go in this ancient kingdom, who care about Scotland. It burns in their souls, and one day I hope they get their hearts' desire.

Introduction

Thee, Caledonia, thy wild heaths among,
Thee, famed for martial deed and sacred Song,
To thee I return with swimming eyes;
Where is that soul of Freedom fled?
(Robert Burns, from stanzas on Liberty, an Ode for General
Washington's birthday)

I LOVE SCOTLAND. It's the country of my birth and I love it unreservedly, but I'm not blinkered to its faults.

I would fight to protect its borders and the lives of its people, my countrymen and women, but I'm not a fanatic – a tunnel-vision nationalist with stupid romantic ideals is something I am not. I do believe, however, that you cannot respect others if you have no self-respect, and for much of its history Scotland has had no self-respect. It has often been the lowest of the low – occupied Europe. A country run by, and dependent upon, another. Its people ruled by another nation.

Every product imported into Scotland makes money for a government centred in London, England.

Whether it is baked beans or toilet paper, some of that money goes to Westminster, where loud is the cry that my people are 'subsidy junkies' who are given more than their fair share.

This nation is held tight in the grasp of a foreign power. We are told that we are a drain on the economy of that 'Union', but the powers that be are loath to let us go.

Let my people go.

When we have self-respect, we can respect and aid others. We can be confident when we have self-respect. We can be proud of our individualism and all that it encompasses.

I hear arguments for internationalism, that the world should live as one. I *do* see the benefits.

But surely we have to begin by obliterating serfdom?

One people having the right of choice over another is not just. Man (and I use that term without sexist overtones, like I would say 'ducks' when I mean ducks and drakes) was born free. But everywhere in the world he is in chains.

There is no real freedom of speech in Scotland. At election times our newspapers tell us for whom we should vote, as if we could not work it out for ourselves – but the press serves its foreign masters. Our television service is extraordinary. We are bombarded with the viewpoints of another nation – football being the prime example. I know it must happen elsewhere in the world, but why do we have to listen to another country extolling its greatness in the sporting arena when we have our own sportsmen and women competing?

As I have said, I love Scotland. I want to see what it is capable of when it has to fend for itself.

Then there would be no one else to blame for any shortcomings.

But what is 'Scotland'? Surely all borders are nothing but man-made boundaries? Birds fly across them without any change of circumstance. Why should a man born a mile north of a man-made boundary be different from one born a mile south of it? I know that the people of Coldstream on the River Tweed (which forms the border between Scotland and England here) are very definitely Scots – but I only have to walk one hundred metres over the connecting bridge and the people of its southern end at Cornhill-on-Tweed are very definitely and identifiably English, even though they have been raised and have intermingled with those on the northern side of the river, perhaps even sharing the same schools and amenities.

Even the Romans sensed the moot change here when they came north – building Hadrian's Wall, a sensed border close to the modern geographical one.

I have no problem with the English, by the way. The English are the English. Some of the best and most loyal friends I have ever had are English – and rightly so. The English are a nation with many redeeming features.

My problem is with the Scots. They have the ability to grasp self-determination. They have the ability to grasp whatever the hell they want. But they don't. Blame lies fully at Scotland's door. It is said the English compromise whereas the Scots don't know the meaning of the word.

The Scots are usually so busy fighting each other that they have never learned to blend together in order to fight anyone else – except at times of leadership of the magnitude of that of King Robert Bruce. It seems to be a fault of Celtic countries in particular. The Irish are even better at infighting than the Scots! Anglo-Saxons seem to cohere and covet neighbouring lands. The English and Germans are both examples of this. But I digress.

None of this explains my love for my native heath.

It is there. It is in my soul and I could no sooner destroy it than fly in the air.

I *am* aware that nothing lasts forever. I know that several million years hence our sun will change. It will go through its own particular life cycle and mutate into what is called a red giant, greatly expanding from the yellow star we have today. As it expands, its outer edge will eventually reach the orbit of Mars. Earth, and Scotland with it, will disappear as rapidly as a sheet of tissue paper dropped in a furnace. I know this. I grasp the reality of it. But I still love Scotland.

The rolling Border country of the Tweed. The view from the mountain tops of the Highlands. The windswept shores of the Hebrides. The very different attitudes of the peoples of her various cities. The yearning still exists. Oh Caledonia. We are your sons and daughters. And we will again be free.

O Canada!

O Canada!
Our home and native land!
True patriot love
in all thy sons command.
With glowing hearts
we see thee rise,
the True North strong and free!
From far and wide,
O Canada,
we stand on guard for thee.
God keep our land
glorious and free!
O Canada,
we stand on guard for thee,
O Canada,
we stand on guard for thee!
(Canadian national anthem)

I HAD FLOWN OVER Canada three times before I eventually set foot there. Don't get me wrong – I'm not a jet-setter. I had never been on a jet before I was thirty – never had the money, to be honest. I had visited the US three times, and the aircraft, due to the curvature of the earth, would fly from Scotland out over the North Atlantic, cross Greenland, then strike land over the northeast reaches of Canada. I would marvel at the amount of ice and snow cover, even with summer approaching, but still more amazing to me after the confines of little Scotland was the distance covered before I could spot a road far below. It seemed like, and probably was, a thousand miles.

My geography is quite good, and I still have a boy-like fascination for scanning the terrain 30,000 feet below with my forehead pressed hard against the glass. The size of the country was not lost on me. Rivers snaked across the seemingly endless panorama of forest. I knew that many of my people had crossed this landscape after their uprooting from their native Scotland. They had paddled these rivers, water being the easiest route into the huge recesses of the Canadian interior.

The New World. A place where those who had been betrayed by the policies inherent in the old could perhaps build better for them and theirs. They were loath to go, of course. When you have been a hundred generations a Scot it is difficult to give your heart, body and soul to a new and unfamiliar terrain. A terrain where the winters were colder and the summers hotter than those you had been bred to. My people, taken from the glen they had been born to. They were the very essence and product of that glen – but sheep were more profitable and the ties of kinship were broken. The Highland Clearances of Scotland are a huge stain spread across our history books.

My actual touching of Canadian soil came about through one Jim Wallace. Jim had read my book *On the Trail of William Wallace*. He is heavily involved in the Clan Wallace Society of North America, and has some say in the Highland Games circuit in Canada. He phoned my publisher in Edinburgh and asked if I could talk as well as I could write, as he wanted me to orate at a couple of the Highland Games and Scottish festivals they have there. One thing led to another, and I travelled out to Canada at the start of August 2001. The first great shock was the heat. It was sweltering, Canada having its hottest spell since 1936. Thirty-eight degrees, 'but more like forty-five degrees with the humidity' stated the news reports. And me in full belted plaid with broadswords and targe too. After five minutes I couldn't have been any wetter if I had jumped in a bath. I drank a lot of alcohol during my time there, but couldn't even feel its effect as I sweated it back out right away. At the bar in one of the tents at a Highland Gathering, the barman said that he had noticed I had consumed quite a lot. I replied that I had seen a poster in Scotland that stated 'Drink Canada Dry' and that I was doing my very best. This caused much hilarity and I realised that the humour that we take for granted in Scotland might just be seen as cutting edge on the other side of the Atlantic.

My first Canadian Highland Games was a revelation: fifty-thousand people, many in kilts, and nearly all of Scots extraction. In fact, many people who approached me in conversation when I first arrived spoke to me in Gaelic. This was a surprise. They were mostly descendants of the Clearances and the language had been passed down the generations. The skilful playing I could hear all around me on pipes and fiddle, the T-shirts people were wearing bearing such slogans as 'If it's no Scottish it's SHITE!' and just the obvious pride in Scottish ancestry made me realise I had walked into something that I did not expect. Everybody I spoke to in the first hour said they or their parents or their grandparents were from Port Glasgow or Helensburgh or Liddesdale or Uist or a myriad of other places which I could immediately picture in my mind's eye.

I have never prepared a speech in my life – I've always just tried to tell an audience what is in my heart and hoped it was enough. Until I walked in front of my first audience at the Games I had no real idea of what I was going to say. I had on my plaid and my weaponry, of course, and I could always explain the clothes and the fighting techniques used, but looking out over the faces the gist of it came to me.

I just did my best to try to put into words what went on inside their hearts and their heads.

I told them how Scotland burned within me, and that I knew it burned within them too, and that the reason for this was that while they might be two, three or four generations a Canadian, they were a Scot one hundred, maybe one thousand generations before that – that their blood went back to the days before Scotland was Scotland. They were the products of that little corner of Europe that seems to instill a passion in the heart and hold its children in a thrall that no other nation on earth can match.

But why does Scotland hold its sons and daughters so? The old clan system still seems to exist, flickering in the soul. The old ties of land and kinship still tug at the hearts of many tens of thousands of Scots exiles the world over. It is expressed in Canada in the many Highland Games and Gatherings scattered over the provinces.

One line seemed to stick with them: the blood is strong.

If I had a pound for every person who came up to me after my first speech who said that that line touched them, I'd have had at least a fiver.

The first Games were held in a little village called Maxville in Ontario. Maxville is a village with a population in the hundreds, not the thousands, but it explodes into a town of tens of thousands for the Games. This area, populated as it is by those of Scots descent, is known as Glengarry, and it is that moniker the games have taken – Glengarry Highland Games. Its speciality is its piping competition, and the final spectacle on the Sunday night is one that will remain with me forever. The sun had just gone down, it was that shady twilight between day and the final onset of night. The sky was huge (Canadian skies seem so much bigger than the skies in hilly Scotland). It was a riot of purple and orange; Venus and Mercury were just starting to show as pinpricks of light against the darkening blue.

Sixty-four pipe bands marched into the floodlit area like a huge army – a sea of tartan, almost like a throwback to the martial glory of times past.

A lone piper stepped forward and played the opening verse of *Amazing Grace*. There was an eerie silence in the vast arena, the sort of quiet I have only heard at football matches at home when a minute's silence is held in memory, and the crowd has hushed to show their respect.

It was thin and clear, the sound of that lone piper, but at the onset of the second verse the many thousands of pipes and drums joined in, in perfect timing; the onslaught to the senses was incredible. Bagpipes have the power to raise the hairs on the back of the neck of most Scots, but this was passion unleashed, a veritable army of Scots blood, playing as one, the twilight sky with its vibrant colours the perfect backdrop. A tear ran. I couldn't help it. All around people were the same. Some were ashen-faced. Many held a handkerchief, dabbing at their faces unashamedly.

I was proud. Sometimes, just sometimes, it really is brilliant to be Scottish.

Canada has its own attractions, of course. Female Mounties were a distraction. I'd like to have taken one home to introduce to the boys down the pub. I had my swords on, but these girls tote guns. I suppose that gives them a feeling of superiority! Shiny boots, too. As a boot-wearer on motorcycles, a well made, well looked-after pair of boots shined to perfection is something that gets noticed. The fact that these were on such perfect specimens of womanhood is neither here nor there.

Another of Canada's attractions is Niagara Falls. I was just getting the barrel with a Saltire painted on it over the fence so I could make my Scottish attempt to ride the falls, when security grabbed me and hauled me back. Sorry people. I did my best.

The grass in Canada is very coarse. I can't speak for the whole country, of course, but certainly in Ontario it was very rough. Most Scots, for some strange reason, when they see sunlight – something quite rare in their home country – go and lie on the nearest bit of grass. Being a creature of habit, I lay on the nearest available stretch whenever I had time off from working, but instead of the soft luxuriant growth of home, I found that after a few minutes my skin could not bear the scratching and itching this grass caused. So beware all Scots tempted to emigrate – take some grass seed with you. If it does not manage to survive the harsh ten feet of snow that the winters there can bring, I would buy a greenhouse or something similar and plant the grass inside it. Just so you can go and have a lie down if you fancy it.

While I was doing my stuff at the Highland Games at Fergus (twinned with Blairgowrie, Perthshire, Scotland!), north-west of Toronto, the boys from the Clan Wallace asked if I would say a few words at their dinner. I was happy to oblige. The dinner was held in the Transylvania Club in Kitchener (honestly!). The foyer had a collection of photos of past presidents of the club on display, and I had this vision where all of these pictures sprouted fangs once the lights were put out at night. I should have looked at the founder just to see if it was Vlad the Impaler. Maybe next year.

The Wallace guys were great. All these Wallaces gathered in one room. The blood of William Wallace must have been among them. A proud name to bear. I found it all quite touching, all these people aware of who they were, aware of the pride their surname carried in a land four thousand miles away.

I was just getting up to make my speech when they nailed me – unintentionally, but they nailed me.

They presented me with a dirk, a beautiful hand-made dirk, in a case with a plaque on the front celebrating my visit. I was already feeling quite emotional. This finished me.

Once I had recovered my poise, I was at least able to start by telling them how William Wallace, warrior as he was, had knelt to shed tears over the body of his comrade, Sir John the Graham, on the battlefield at Falkirk.

Perhaps that is a trait of Celtic blood. I'm six-feet-five and have trained in gyms most of my life. I'm used to wielding medieval weaponry. I often describe myself as 'not very bright, but I enjoy lifting heavy things', yet I can be reduced to tears as much as I can be roused to violence, or at least the threat of it!

Bloody Scots, too busy fighting each other to get on with uniting to combat the real issues, but equally morose when it comes to celebrating the military defeats in their chequered history. Thanks for the dirk, boys!

Whilst in Canada I did some bits and pieces for television. I got a phone call from City TV in Toronto, enquiring as to whether I had brought my motorcycle with me. I replied that I had too much trouble trying to get it up the stairs to the aircraft and unfortunately had to leave it behind at Glasgow Airport. Oh, they replied, then we will hire you one so we can have you on a bike for the show. And hire me one they did.

A guy turned up on 1500 cc of Indian motorcycle. It was all pure grunt, and not a lot else. There's me in kilt and weapons, shades on, riding this in Toronto. I got a row for not wearing a helmet – it's unsafe, don't you know? But I was wearing broadswords! Rode the bike into the studio, cameras rolling. The interview could not have gone better if I had staged it all beforehand. I could not believe it when the host asked me: 'What's worn under the kilt?' The perfect opportunity to use the old chestnut 'nothing, it's all in perfect working order'! The studio audience definitely hadn't heard it before. Seems everybody saw the show as I was recognised constantly after that.

Canada was a revelation in lots of ways. The Scottishness of the gatherings is astounding. The number of expat Scots is astounding. But they are lucky.

They are able to take all the good things about Scotland and put it on show, without the baggage of the bad.

Pageantry galore. Caber-tossing, piping, dancing, history, pride, and a very attuned sense of self.

No bigotry, damp housing, heroin problems, and no living in a second-class nation. And although much drink was being consumed, I saw no one out of control or being abusive.

When the arenas emptied at the end of these events there was no litter to speak of. I realised on my return to Scotland just how filthy our towns and cities can be. I often see individuals drop litter, even as they are walking by litter bins. I have never been afraid to point this out to the culprits, usually because I am big enough and ugly enough to get away with it, but I am met with uncomprehending expressions at the best of times. Selfish unthinking wastes of oxygen that somebody else could be breathing.

The worst is when the culprits are children accompanied by an adult and the parent says nothing. I feel at these moments it would be a good idea to pass a law that allows you to kick offenders up the backside with all necessary force. In the meantime I suppose I will have to put up with the rubbish blown onto our grass verges and into hedges.

It has been said that it is the ones who were left behind at the Clearances who were the unlucky ones. Perhaps there is some truth in that. Life would have been hard, but generations on they seem, on the surface at least, to have made for themselves the best of a bad start here in Canada. The standard of living is superb.

So why don't you go and live there then, I hear you ask.

It might look Scottish, with the water and the trees. The Scottish festivals and Games are on a scale we can only dream of here. But the bottom line is this: it isn't Scotland. And my heart is very firmly rooted in Scotland, complete with all its faults. I've seen how it could be. Canada showed me that. And surely pride and change here are worth the fight.

Language. It's a funny thing, language. I thought the Canadians spoke the same language as the Scots. Oh, except for the French Canadians.

I found early in my trip that this was not the case. First day, I went into the mall in Cornwall. Purchased a watch that was ridiculously cheap. Not surprising, really: it stopped the next day. At least it was right twice a day. Somewhere in the conversation with the lady who sold me it, I happened to mention Toronto. She laughed and asked me to say that again.

Tor-on-toe, I obliged. She laughed again and said I was welcome to stand and say it all day to keep her smiling. I didn't really get it at first. I know how it is written. It says Toronto on the maps. I say that *Tor-on-toe*. It seems that it does not say that to Canadians. They see the word Toronto on the map too, but when they say it, it has the first 'o' and the last 't' missing. *Trono*. Same word, different sound. *Tor-on-toe* sounds like the Lone Ranger's sidekick. I had noticed something similar on a trip to Chicago. Scots seem to slip an 'r' into that one. *Chi-car-go*. Or maybe even *Chi-carrr-go*.

It has been said that 'Britain' and North America are separated by a common language. This may be so. I do notice Americans tend to put the stress on a different syllable from the Scots. We say LANark. They say LanARK. Let's call the whole thing off!

There is one other matter to be cleared up at this point. In the introduction to *On the Trail of Bonnie Prince Charlie* I wrote that my favourite drink (other than Belgian beer) is whisky and lemonade.

I was approached by several people in Canada who said that they had tried it – and that it was disgusting.

Allow me to explain.

I had no idea whilst writing that my books, containing very much a Scottish bent, would eventually sell in other countries. They had mixed the whisky (or confusingly, as they call it, 'Scotch') with *their* lemonade, which is made from freshly squeezed lemons. I must admit, putting that in whisky sounds hideous. I meant, of course, the lemonade we have in Scotland, consisting of various chemicals in a clear solution which has probably never been near a lemon in its life, or, at the very most, was perhaps accidentally held near a lemon for a while.

I'll need to be careful about what I write in future. I don't want people thinking I'm crazier than I am already!

Who Are the Scots?

MOST SCOTS PROBABLY think very little of the past. Yes, if pressed they would be able to talk a little of their heroes from times past, like Wallace or Bruce. Some may be able to delve a little further and name others of the calibre of the great Montrose. Some may be able to slip back into hallowed antiquity and mention Calgacus. But where did this brawling, questing people called the Scots originally come from?

You would probably be lucky to find one Scot in a thousand who could elucidate on that question.

Where do countries come from anyway? What seed is planted to begin the growing process of a people?

Apart from modern nations like the USA or Australia, many of the older countries of the world would have started like a 'gang'. Individuals, knowing that they were vulnerable to attack or theft, would have joined into co-operatives with others, perhaps with blood ties, in a union of sorts. Obviously, a group would be harder to assail than an individual, and these groups would unite to form a general offensive policy against aggressors.

Touch one, touch all, no less. As time passed, these groups would inter-marry and tribes were born. From such lowly backgrounds, nations and peoples came into being.

So where did kings come from?

I suppose, if we think about it, somewhere in the distant past of any royal family there was an individual who was what we Scots would term 'a bad bastard'. Someone who had the muscle power to cow those around him. Perhaps there would be an argument over the ownership of some sheep. One of the claimants would perhaps stab the other, then turn to his fellows and ask, 'Anybody else want some of this?' So the aggressor then becomes a leader. From such humble beginnings came great European dynasties. From such early days came the much sought after 'royal blood'.

There would be exceptions, of course. Perhaps some leaders emerged because of their intelligence. Brain and not brawn would have given them great leadership qualities. It was only a matter of time until leadership became hereditary. Thus, royalty. The 'bad bastard' theory probably applies to most of what we call 'nobility', too.

To find the initial planting of seeds that eventually grew to become what we know today as the Scots, and their eventual home, Scotland, we have to look into the pages of our earliest chronicles. There is no hard fact, unfortunately, so we can only go by what our early scribes tell us. Legends have to be ignited by some spark, so this is the best we have, and who can refute or deny the rights and wrongs of these legends?

In ancient Greece there resided one Gaythelos, a prince no less. This Gaythelos managed to fall out with his family, due to various cruel and warlike acts he had committed.

Owing to the fact that his family was in a huff, he made his way to Egypt. It was the time of Pharaoh Chencres, and Chencres had a daughter, one Scota, with whom Gaythelos fell in love. This is the origin of the name 'the Scots'. Gaythelos and Scota were married, and their followers, a matriarchal people (like the Celts), adopted Scota's name and called themselves 'Scots', the followers of Scota.

I should explain the idea of Celts being a matriarchal society. I suppose it makes perfect sense, really. There could always be doubt about who the father was when a child's parentage was called into question, but there could never be any doubt about the mother's identity.

The story of Scota is always one I have liked to tell schoolkids when I am doing my stuff in school. It gives the girls a good sense of superiority when they discover their country – and their countrymen – have taken their name from a woman. Scota. The 'first' Scot.

Legend states that Pharaoh Chencres was the man whose armies were destroyed by the waters rushing back after the parting of the Red Sea. After this stroke, which wiped out most of the ruling class of Egypt in one go, there were peasant uprisings all over the land.

Gaythelos, Scota and their followers struck west to escape this trouble. They wandered through the wilderness of North Africa, where one of their number, Jacob by name, wandered off by himself. He rested his head on a stone and drifted off to sleep. He had a dream wherein he saw the angels ascending and descending from heaven. When he returned to the fold of the rest of the Scots, he told them of this. They decided that they would carry this stone pillow with them, and wherever it rested would be the place from where they would be ruled.

I can remember being told this story at primary school. Not the Scots connection, of course. When I was at primary school, Scotland was an entity that was very seldom mentioned. But I certainly remember the story of Jacob and his dream whilst resting his head on pillow of stone. This stone was carried forward by the Scots, and today is better known by its almost mythological name – The Stone of Destiny.

The Scots came through the 'Pillars of Hercules', a geological feature that we know today as the Straits of Gibraltar, and made their way towards Ireland. Perhaps they settled for a while in France *en route*, and that would account for the Celts inherent there today – the Bretons.

The Scots settled in Ireland, their Stone, 'Jacob's Pillow', still safe in their keeping.

But of course from the very north of Ireland they could see another country, even wetter and colder than the one they currently inhabited. Nothing would do but to make a move over the water to settle in Argyll, so the move came in the sixth century, and the Scots finally arrived in what we now know as Scotland, although to those with the Gaelic it has always been Alba, home of the Albannach.

The Stone was brought with them, of course, to settle with them in its new home. Where it resides is where the Scots are ruled from. It moved house several times over the coming centuries, Scone in Perthshire becoming its eventual spiritual home, this explaining why it is sometimes called the 'Stone of Scone'.

The Scots made their early settlements grouped around their fortress at Dunadd, a great rocky outcrop rising from A'Mhoine Mhor, the Great Moss, near Lochgilphead.

There are interesting carvings that can still be seen at the remains of the rocky fort of Dunadd. A footprint carved into the solid rock, and an outline of a wild boar, are the two most promi-nent. It is believed that Scots paying homage to their king could bring some of their own soil with them to pour into the footprint, so that the act of fealty could be taken with their foot inserted into the hollow, the oath taken as if they were standing on their own soil. The footprint, carved in the living rock, also shows the symbolism between man and the actual ground of Scotland. The outline of the boar is the symbol of the ancient Scots, their badge or banner no less, and this was in use right up to the time of William I of Scotland, who reigned from 1165 to 1214.

The influence of the Scots was soon to permeate across the country they had chosen for their own.

There were already people settled in Scotland, of course. The Picts, another Celtic race, had settled when the ice retreated at the end of the last ice age. They, like the Scots, were aware of the signifi-cance of stone in a country that had plenty of it, and parts of Scotland today are still covered by the legacy the Picts left behind – standing stones, burial cairns and carven rocks.

The standing stones at Callanish on the island of Lewis were old when the pyramids were built, and before most civilizations were even thought of the people here were already charting the changing seasons, using the course of the stars.

Pictish history in Scotland predates the arrival of the Scots, and it was the Picts, of course, who withstood the invasion of the Roman Empire.

It's the appearance of the Romans that brings an intriguing fact down the centuries to us. The Romans had with them a scribe called Tacitus, and he recorded the goings-on of those times. Tacitus tells us the name of the very first inhabitant of Scotland ever recorded: Calgacus the swordsman. Calgacus was the leader of the tribes of Scotland who had united to counter the Roman threat.

And not only is Calgacus the first inhabitant we know by name, he is also the first whose words have come down to us.

According to Tacitus, at a meeting with the Romans, Calgacus is said to have made the defiant comment, 'You Romans come here, create a desert and call it peace.' Stirring words indeed to echo down through the ages. Unfortunately, Calgacus was slain at the battle of Mons Graupius, where the tribes of Scotland, which the Romans named Caledonia, were soundly defeated with great slaughter. The site of Mons Graupius has long been a matter of debate between historians. Mons Graupius was to have another effect upon Scotland, however, as it is from this battle that the Grampian Mountains take their name. A spelling error, where the battle was written as 'Grampius' rather than 'Graupius', was the root of this, and so Grampian stuck.

The Romans could not subdue the Caledonian peoples, and brought forward the Ninth or Hispanic Legion to quell their aggressiveness. The Ninth marched north, only to disappear. The site of their unrecorded massacre is unknown.

During a holiday in Majorca, I took an interest in the history of the place. I'm afraid history permeates me everywhere I go, and I always want to know what has happened in the landscapes I am exploring. Majorca, being a Mediterranean island, has seen many of the great civilisations come and go, like the Romans or Phoenicians. Reading a local history book, while visiting the remains of a Moorish stronghold, a line jumped out at me. It stated that during the Roman occupation, Majorca was noted for its slingers, or stones thrown from slings, as in David and Goliath.

It said that a company of these slingers was raised, and comprised a section of the Ninth, the Hispanic Legion.

The same section which tried, and died, in its attempt to conquer little Scotland.

Funny how history twists and turns. So many Scots go to Majorca for their summer holidays, many, many thousands every year. It seems strange that two thousand years ago many of the young men of this island travelled half way across the known world to attempt to conquer my homeland for their Roman masters. Perhaps my taxi driver, or my barman that day, are descendants of men who had seen service in Caledonia. The modern-day islanders never give it a thought, obviously, nor do my country-folk on their holidays. But we are all part of the same complex spiral, and I'm sure that the members of the Ninth Legion left behind some of their blood in the melting pot of Scotland. Latin lovers may not just be in the domain of modern women's magazines!

The Emperor Hadrian decided that a great wall should be

built to keep these unruly Caledonians under control. And built it was, from Solway to Tyne, seventy miles of forts and towers. When I see it, and think of the guards who stood at the top of it scanning the country to the north, it makes me wonder at the martial ability and defiance of my ancestors. The Romans had conquered Europe, parts of Asia, and even the north of Africa, but this little scrap of land on the edge of the world required a wall to be built.

I actually felt quite proud when I went to the cinema to see *Gladiator* when it was released in 2000, and a message appeared at the start that proclaimed: 'At the height of its power the Roman Empire was vast, stretching from the deserts of Africa to the borders of Northern England.'

Aye, build a wall!

I do often wonder why they wanted to roam so far from the sultry climes of the Mediterranean to the incessant drizzle of Scotland. Perhaps they thought we had deposits of oil in the North Sea or something.

I remember one wee snippet that intrigues me, where Hadrian's Wall is concerned. When upgrading work was taking place on the M74, a stretch, not too far north of Hadrian's Wall, was contracted out to an Italian construction firm. It turned out that it took them longer to build a stretch of motorway, with diggers, excavators and all the paraphernalia of modern machinery, than it had taken the Romans to build an equivalent length of wall, with its ditches, ramparts and supply roads. And the Romans had nothing more mechanical than a basic wheelbarrow!

So much for two thousand years of technology. The Romans did push forward from their frontier, of course, building the Antonine Wall from Forth to Clyde, across that narrow waist of Scotland. It was held, on and off, for only forty years, the tribes of the north managing to overrun it several times before it was eventually abandoned. Often I have stood at some of the well-preserved sections near Bonnybridge, looking north to the Campsie and Ochil Hills and wondering what terrors they held for the garrisons here.

A bizarre legend has 'done the rounds' in Scotland for many years: that Pontius Pilate, he who ordered the crucifixion of Jesus, was born in Scotland. The Romans had a forward frontier post at Fortingall in Perthshire, and it is said that Pilate was born here. I have heard it claimed that archives have revealed that Pilate's father was part of the occupying forces of Scotland at one time, so maybe the legend is true.

Scots like to claim that they invented anything worth inventing – Scots invented television, the telephone, road surfacing and so on – so perhaps in a roundabout way they actually invented Christianity too!

Certainly the oldest tree in Europe, a venerable Yew, stands in Fortingall. It is so ancient it would be able to recall the days of the coming of the Romans.

The Roman Empire started to crumble and contract, finally leaving us around 400AD. There is very little recorded evidence for the following centuries, the Pictish people of Scotland leaving only their carven stones in mute testament to their existence. There are legends, though, such as that of Arthur of the Britons, possibly a member of the race that inhabited what we know today as Strathclyde. Many places in Scotland are pointed out as the scenes of his actions. The Round Table stands at Stirling, Merlin is buried at Drummelzier in Tweeddale, Guinevere is buried at Meigle, Camelot is Camelon, an old fort-site near Falkirk, and so on. It's just that the English have hijacked the stories and based the whole thing there!

In the years after 500AD the Scots began to permeate into western Scotland. There was fighting between Scot and Pict, but intermingling and intermarriage caused a fusion between the peoples, culminating in the reign of Kenneth MacAlpin, beginning in 843AD, whom we regard today as the first king of what we can identify as Scotland. Kenneth was of the line of the Kings of the Scots, and may have been heir to the Pictish throne through his mother. It was Kenneth who transferred the Stone of Destiny to Scone, and it became the crowning place of the Kings of Scots.

It should be pointed out that it is King of Scots, and not King of Scotland – and there is a vast difference. The crown in Scotland rests on the head of the people, so to speak. The Scots only have Scotland for one lifetime each, almost like it is rented. They don't own the land. They are only lucky enough to live in it. And the

monarch is no different. King of the Scots, not of the land.
And the Stone of Destiny?

The Stone we have today just looks like the sandstone that occurs in the Scone area. Many have been the theories that say Edward Longshanks of England did not take the real stone when he invaded Scotland in 1296. The Abbot of Scone supposedly switched it, keeping the original safe. If so, where is the original today? I am often asked by audiences if I know the whereabouts of the Stone. Conspiratorially, I ask if they can keep a secret – it's under my bed.

Stone aficionados should search for a copy of Pat Gerber's *The Search for the Stone of Destiny* – it at least lays down all the legend and possibilities. I bought a copy when it first came out, but it has been superseded by an edition with an extra chapter covering the return of the Stone to Scotland in 1996. Being Scottish, I was loath to spend money on buying another copy, so I read the extra chapter standing in a bookshop. I read the part that talked about the Stone crossing the centre of the bridge over the Tweed at Coldstream, and how a kilted figure in the trees cried 'Freedom!' as this historic event took place. I hate to say this, but that kilted figure was me.

The old legends state that wherever the Stone is kept, from there the Scots will be ruled. It came back in 1996. By 1997 the Scots had voted for their own parliament. Maybe the magic is still there. Even if it only is a block of Scone sandstone graced by seven hundred years of English royal arses.

King James VI used to like telling his English courtiers, after he had inherited that country's throne, that Gaelic was the language spoken in the Garden of Eden. Perhaps he was not wrong. Gaelic is similar in form to Sanskrit – a language of the east. Perhaps the old chronicles tell the truth of the origins of the Scots.

On the Trail of the Tombs of the Kings

Great Caesar, now dead and gone away,
Is but dust to fill a hole to keep the wind away

WHEN I WAS NINETEEN, I played guitar in a band. I was in London hawking my demo tapes around the various record companies, hoping for the elusive deal. I dreamed of having top-ten success – and I eventually achieved it, but I did it in the Scottish book charts instead, proving that my pen was mightier than my Fender Stratocaster. I had time to kill, so I paid a visit to Westminster Abbey. I have always had a hankering for history, and although I love Scotland with all my body and soul, ancient buildings in any city or country attract me like a magnet.

Westminster Abbey is the last resting place of most of England's royalty, and as I surveyed these phalanxes of tombs, it made me think of Scotland, and that there is no equivalent here. Where were all the kings and queens of Scots spending their eternal rest? I knew that many of the early ones were buried on Iona. I knew that Robert the Bruce was buried in Dunfermline, as I had seen his tomb in the abbey on a family visit while I was still at school. But where were all the others? I had some knowledge of Scots history at that age, but not enough to have named all the royal line from, say, 1000AD onward – that all came later.

Most of the information regarding the last resting places of the Scots kings was gleaned by accident. I would come across them while covering Scotland by my preferred mode of transport, my motorcycle, or I would discover a reference, usually no more than a line or two, in a history book. The tombs were scattered between different religious buildings all over Scotland and I began to realise that there was a gap in the history of my nation, because no one seems ever to have listed them before. Historians I have spoken to have generally known where a couple were buried, but I have never met anyone who knew where they all were.

I have named this chapter 'On the Trail of the Tombs of the Kings' simply because Scotland has only ever had one reigning queen – the world-famous Mary Queen of Scots. Margaret, the little maid of Norway, whose death sparked the Wars of Independence, died in Orkney, and although she was the rightful queen, she never actually reigned over her kingdom. I have included these two, along with all the queen consorts whose last resting places I could locate, but apart from Mary all Scotland's rulers were male. Nothing sexist in this, of course. As I've already mentioned, the Scots are a Celtic people, and the Celts were generally matriarchal in matters of lineage. The ruler in Scotland, however, was not only expected to reign over his people but was also expected to be a battle commander, so sons were generally chosen over elder sisters. But is it a job that anyone would really have wanted? Reading through these pages will bring home the fact that very few of Scotland's kings died in their beds. Cold steel seems to have been the lot of most.

This chapter is about more than just tombs, however. Visiting these places becomes more poignant when you discover how these people met their end and some of those ends were bizarre indeed. Some of these kingly remains had strange things happen to them long after their deaths. Very few of our medieval rulers have lain undisturbed since their interment, and I have done my best to uncover all the strange tales that I could find. Everybody likes a touch of the macabre, don't they? But I wanted this to be fun too. The map at the front of this book shows where these people are interred, and I hope it will spur the mobile among you to go and have a look at some of these tombs. After all, the dust there is all that remains of what were, in their lifetime, the most powerful people in their country, people who saw the great events of our history take place, people who commanded at our greatest victories, and who witnessed the slaughter at our most notorious defeats.

However, it must be borne in mind that in their day these people could boast the proud title King, or Queen, of Scots, and Scotland is arguably the oldest nation state in the world. So why are they so scattered? It seems that Scotland has spent much of its long existence fighting off inroads from its aggressive neighbour, and rulers were buried in the place that seemed most expedient at the time.

Few tombs stand in buildings that are still intact. Our land-scape is scattered with picturesque ruins that once were awe-inspiring structures of beauty. Those which were not burnt by invading English armies were destroyed by the Scots themselves, fired up with zeal at the time of the Reformation. The preachers incited the masses to smash everything they could find that smacked of idolatry, and unfortunately many ornate tombs came under that remit, and were destroyed by the mob. These abbey-burners thought that they were righteous as they set about their orgies of destruction, but they wiped out so many buildings which, still standing, would have added to the wonders of the world, packed with treasures of every era of Scotland's story.

But hindsight is a wonderful thing, and as we Scots soldier on I can only hope that we can learn from the past. If this chapter goes a little way towards helping with that learning process, then it will have been worth all the endorsements I have accrued on my licence while motorcycling around the country at a great rate of knots in order to gather all the necessary information. As so many of our earliest rulers were buried on Iona, I shall start by listing the tombs there as a separate entity.

Part I: Iona

Iona stands about a mile distant from the south-west corner of the island of Mull. It is about three-and-a-half miles long by a mile-and-a-half wide, and its highest point is Dun-I, which rises to a height of 327 feet.

This island first appears in our history books with its associ-ations with St Columba (in the Gaelic he is known as Columcille). Columba was an Irish princeling, who from boyhood was noted for his piety and devotion to wisdom. About the year 545AD he is said to have founded a large monastery in Ireland. This incident led to two of the great tribes of Ireland rising in confrontation. Columba incited the northern Hy Neill to attack the southern Hy Neill, and these two clans came to battle at Culdremline in Connaught in 561, where Columba's northern Hy Neill defeated their southern counterparts with great slaughter, after a long and bloody battle. Columba was later held responsible for this carnage. It was said that he had incurred help through his prayers to the Almighty for this victory.

Whether by forceful expulsion or by dint of his conscience, Columba decided to leave Ireland, sailing until it was out of sight. He would then settle and try to convert as many of the locals from paganism as possible, in atonement for his part in the battle.

Columba set out from Ireland in 563 at the age of forty-two and made for the Western Isles of Scotland. He made landings at Islay, Jura and Colonsay, but found that Ireland was visible from all on a clear day. He then landed on Iona on 12 May, traditionally at the bay now known as Port-a-churaich, and when he discovered that Ireland was no longer visible, he settled down to begin his good works.

Columba and his followers were to be responsible for spreading the word of God over much of Scotland, even eventually managing to convert some of the pagan English. His earthly life came to an end on Iona itself. He breathed his last there on 9 June 597, and a shrine was built over his last resting place, but like so many contained within these pages he was moved several times due to various incursions by Viking raiders.

Iona, as you can imagine, was particularly accessible to these raiders due to its sea-girt position. Columba's time here ensured that Iona became thought of as some kind of cradle of Christianity, and as Christians felt that burial here would perhaps ensure them a place in heaven it became inevitable that it would become the last resting place of royalty. And come they did.

Iona is reputedly the last resting place of no fewer than forty-eight kings of Scotland, and they are joined by four kings of Ireland and eight kings of Norway. The flat-lying grave slabs that mark their resting places are contained within the burial ground known as the Reilig Odhrain.

Legend states that it is so called because it was believed that the ground could not be consecrated without a sacrificial burial. Columba asked for a volunteer from among his followers, and one Odhrain (pronounced 'Oran') stepped forward. He was buried alive. Possibly this was some throwback to Druidicial ways, as the early Celts often marked the foundation of buildings with some sort of sacrificial burial. Columba had him dug up after three days, whereupon Odhrain told the bystanders that 'there was neither deity nor devil, nor future happiness nor future punishment' – words which so shocked Columba that he immediately had Odhrain reburied!

When Dr Samuel Johnson and James Boswell visited Iona during their tour of the Hebrides in 1773, Boswell remarked, 'There are only some gravestones flat on the earth, and we could see no inscriptions. How far short was this of marble monuments, like those in Westminster Abbey, which I had imagined here!'

So it seems I am not the only one who has looked at the serried ranks of tombs at Westminster and made a Scottish comparison. Much of the stonework and many inscriptions here at Iona, however, have been defaced over the centuries by relic seekers, never mind the legacy of repeated Viking raids!

There is another interesting wee insight into Iona in the 1500s, when it was visited by Donald Munro, Dean of the Isles, who left an account of his visit. According to Munro, there were three tombs formed like chapels, in which were laid the 'kings of three fair realms'. The first, which contained the kings from Fergus II to Macbeth, was inscribed *Tumulus Regum Scotiae*, the second, which contained the remains of four Irish kings, had the inscription *Tumulus Regum Hiberniae*, and the third, with eight Norwegian kings, was marked *Tumulus Regum Norwegiae*. Certainly these three chapel-like tombs have entirely disappeared, and only the flat tombstones remain. Dean Munro's statement that Macbeth was the last king to be buried on Iona is wrong. Two were buried here after the death of Macbeth.

But who were these many kings who lie for eternity on Iona? There are supposedly forty-eight kings of Scots within the Reilig Odhrain. This is possibly a true figure. The earlier thirty are believed to be the kings of Dalriada, the area of the western seaboard first colonised by the Scots after they crossed from Ireland. The later eighteen are all true kings of Scots, territorial gains having taken place for our modern concept of the Scottish nation to have evolved. We know a little about some of these kings from scant mentions within old chronicles.

Bruide, who was king of the Picts and a convert to

Christianity, died in the year 693, and was taken to Iona for burial. Columba was dead by this time and his successor was named Adamnan. A strange tale is recorded in the *Life of Adamnan*, which was compiled in the tenth century in Ireland, where it relates that Adamnan attempted to raise the dead by bringing Bruide back to life. When his body began to stir, and the eyes began to flicker, one of the other monks begged Adamnan to desist, as all his successors would not seem worthy if they could not emulate this feat. Adamnan saw the sense in this, and let Bruide's soul depart to heaven.

Kenneth MacAlpin, who is credited with being the first king of our modern ideal of Scotland, is also buried on Iona. He died at Forteviot, a few miles south-west of Perth. An old gazetteer mentions:

> On a small eminence now called the Halyhill, at the west end of the village, over-hanging May water, stood Fortevieth, the ancient capital of Fortrenn. According to legend, Angus MacFergus, King of the Picts (731–61) here built a church, and in his palace here Kenneth MacAlpin died in 860.

Other sources claim MacAlpin's death as having taken place in 858.

After Kenneth's death, the throne of Scotland was filled by his half-brother, **Donald MacAlpin**. In this era of our history, brothers were sometimes given precedence over sons when it came to the succession. I can only assume this was because of age, perhaps because of a son's infancy. But it created rival dynastic claims to the throne of Scotland which often resulted in bloodshed on a grand scale. Perhaps it was a catch-22 situation. If the infant sons were allowed the crown, perhaps their jealous uncles would still have used military might to try and wrest it from them, so the situation would have remained the same. Anyway, Donald was only on the throne for a few years, as he was stabbed to death at his fort at the mouth of the River Almond opposite Scone in 862AD, and was taken to Iona for burial.

After Donald's death, his nephew, Kenneth MacAlpin's son, mounted the throne as **Constantine I**. He reigned for sixteen years. His end came in 877AD after a battle at Dollar against the

Vikings, where the Scots were heavily defeated and had to flee north-eastwards.

Constantine was caught by the northmen at Inverdovat and was slain. His body was then taken to Iona for burial. He was succeeded by his brother, **Aed**, who incidentally is called 'Heth' in John of Fordun's chronicle. He was to last only a few months before being slain at the Battle of Strathallan in 878.

One train of thought places this battle at Blairinroar (the Gaelic Blar-an-roinn, or Battle of Division) as upright stones and stone coffins have been found at the farm of the same name. This Blairinroar stands in the pass that runs between Strathallan and Glen Artney, but the name could refer to a battle fought in this vicinity against the Romans. No matter where this fight took place, Aed's body was afterwards conveyed to Iona for burial.

Aed was succeeded by **Giric**, who managed to remain on the throne of Scotland for twelve years before he died at Dundurn, a fort on the River Earn near St Fillans in 890. As you will no doubt already have guessed, he was shipped to Iona for burial.

Donald II, King of Scots, was next in line. He reigned for eleven years, before dying at Forres in the Great Glen. The Chronicle of the Kings said he died of 'sickness', but the chronicles of John of Fordun, written in the late fourteenth century, say that poison may have been used. He too was buried at Iona.

Donald II's successor, **Constantine** II breaks the chain in having been buried elsewhere. He reigned for forty years, a good length of time for the days of which we speak. He 'abdicated' from the throne in 943 to spend his 'retirement' as a monk at St Andrews, and when he passed away in 952 he was buried somewhere in the precincts of what we know today as St Andrew's Cathedral.

The Chronicle of John of Fordun states that monks from Iona later 'dug up his bones, and took them away and buried them in the tomb of his fathers, in the chapel of the blessed Orain.'

Malcolm, the first King of Scots to bear that name, inherited Constantine II's throne. His end came when he led an army north to deal with an insurrection in the region of Moray, the two sides meeting near Dunnottar at a place one chronicle identifies as 'Ulrim', and another as Fetteresso. He was then transferred to Columba's isle, and buried in 954.

Next up was **King Indulf**, who managed to reign for nine years. His end came in a battle against the Vikings at Cullen in Banffshire. The story has come down to us that Indulf was pursuing the fleeing Vikings back to their ships on the shore at Cullen when he was struck on the head by a dart fired from one of the longships. John of Fordun states, 'His body was taken away to Columba's isle with such honour as was meet, and buried with his forefathers in the customary tomb of the kings.' This took place in 962.

As you can see from the story so far, a bloody end seemed to have been the lot of most who sat upon the throne of Scotland, and the next on the list was to be no exception. **Dubh**, or Duff as he was sometimes known, reigned for four-and-a-half years. His death came in 966. He was probably slain by the man who was to next sit on the Scottish throne, one Culen (nothing to do with the afore-mentioned Banffshire town!).

After Dubh's death a strange story is told in the chronicles. Apparently his body was put in a shallow grave under 'a certain bridge' near Kinloss, and from that moment on darkness shrouded the whole kingdom. The sun only began to shine again when his body was found. Perhaps there was an eclipse at this time and this is how it was perceived by the chroniclers, as in medieval times eclipses were often thought to be harbingers of some major event.

It is mentioned that Dubh's body was put in its coffin embalmed with aromatic spices, before its transfer to Iona. It was probably already badly decomposed and the aromatic spices would at least have made life more bearable for the entourage who had to carry the body right across Scotland to its last resting place.

Culen, his successor, also reigned for four-and-a-half years. He was useless and slack in the government of his kingdom. The chronicles mention that he was 'sore given to violating maids'. He went too far when he took the daughter of one of his noblemen against her will, and on hearing of this her father, named Radhard, found Culen and killed him 'to the great joy of many, and the grief of very few'. This deed is said to have taken place somewhere in Lothian. Although Culen was little loved, the idea of the king being entombed on Iona was obviously well entrenched in the psyche of the nation, as Culen was to be laid in the Relig Odhrain alongside his ancestors.

Next in line was another Kenneth, the second king of Scots to bear that name. This one lasted a good length of time, reigning for twenty-four years before his murder in 995. This **Kenneth** II's end is another which has a strange ring to it. Being king automatically attracted the usual entourage of enemies, and Kenneth II's enemies plotted his downfall in the following manner: The old chronicles tell of a certain female, Finele, who lured the king into her cottage while he was out hunting near the village of Fettercairn. She had a statue of a boy in her house, which had several 'tripwires' leading to crossbows hidden within the room. If the statue was moved, the bolts would be released, aimed to strike whoever was standing before it. The king, once inside the house, enquired about the statue. Finele told him, 'If the top of the head of this statue be touched or moved, a marvellous and pleasant jest comes of it.' The king, of course, stepped forward and moved the statue, only to be transfixed by arrows on either side. Finele slipped out a side door, and it was only when the king's bodyguard became concerned by his non appearance and smashed in the door that the crime was discovered.

The chronicle of John of Fordun states:

> They consumed Fettercairn with fire, knowing not what to do, and reduced it to ashes. Then, taking with them the king's blood-stained body, they shortly afterwards buried it with his fathers in Iona, as was the custom of the kings.

Constantine III was then crowned king, but he lasted a mere eighteen months before he met a gory end in 997, at what could be the fort at the mouth of the Almond near Scone, or on the banks of the Almond in Lothian. (The common river name Almond is a corruption of the Gaelic word for river – *abhainn*. This is also the reason behind so many rivers in Scotland being named the Avon.) Constantine III was taken over land and sea to Iona to spend eternity.

The next reign is a little confusing. For the next eight years

Scotland would seem to have been ruled by a joint father-and-son kingship, the father being **Kenneth III** and the son being **Giric II**. Not only did these two rule together, they also died together, at a battle fought at 'The Moor of the Barde' – Mozievaird in Strathearn, in 1005. There is mention of Giric II being taken to Iona for burial, but none pertaining to Kenneth III, but if the son was carried all that distance, surely the father, who died alongside him, would have been taken too?

The next king, **Malcolm II**, reigned for thirty years, and was the victor of Carham, a mighty battle fought on the River Tweed. He was still fighting at the age of eighty in 1034, when he was wounded in a fight, dying of his injuries at Glamis three days later. After his burial at Iona he was succeeded by his grandson **Duncan**, who hung on to the title of king for six years before being wounded in battle on 15 August 1040 at Pitgaveny, where-upon he was carried to nearby Elgin where he died. Apparently he was slain by the famous Macbeth, but the actual circumstances bear no resemblance to the Shakespearean play. Shakespeare did get one bit right, though, when he has Rosse pose the question, 'Where is Duncan's body?' to which Macduff replies, 'Carried to Colme-kill [Columba's Isle], The sacred storehouse of his prede-cessors, And guardian of their bones.'

Macbeth was crowned king in Duncan's stead and ruled for seventeen years, even making a pilgrimage to Rome during that time, but he, like so many already mentioned, died by the sword, in a fight at Lumphanan in the Earldom of Mar, on 15 August 1057.

Macbeth was followed to the throne by **Lulach**, his stepson, but he lasted a mere four months. He was hunted down by his enemies, eventually being despatched at Essie in Strathbogie, Aberdeenshire, by the man to succeed him as king, the later Malcolm III, in the first few days of the year 1058. Even though Lulach had reigned for such a short term, he was, like Macbeth before him, buried in the hallowed ground of Iona.

The Malcolm III mentioned above, or, as he is more famously known, **Malcolm Canmore** (from the Gaelic *ceann-mor*, or big head – it might mean that he was a wise man, or just that he had a big head) was not interred at Iona, so we will skip over his reign here. He was followed by **Donald III**, who reigned for only six months before being expelled from the throne by **Duncan II**. We'll return to Donald III in a moment.

Duncan II managed to hold on to his rocky throne for six months, till he was slain in 1094 at Mondynes near Stonehaven by the Earl of the Mearns. After his transfer to Iona, the throne was retaken by Donald III, who managed to hang on for another three years, before an army led by Edgar, future King of Scots, captured him and put out his eyes. He was later put to death at Rescobie, near Forfar, in 1097.

Donald III was first buried in Dunkeld, but was later dug up and transferred to Iona. The date of this act is unknown, but it could not have been later than 1150. Donald was the last of the kings to be buried in Iona, among his many ancestors. His descendants would be scattered all over Scotland, occupying various sites in religious houses over the face of the country.

From Fergus, the first king of the tribe called Scots who settled in Argyll, to James VI, the last king to reign over Scotland as a separate entity, sixty-three kings had succeeded each other in one thousand, one hundred years. Forty-eight lie on Iona.

Some of the problems of transportation in what must have been troubled times, to get these rulers to their last resting places across mountainous countryside, must have been immense. No roads, just muddy tracks, and there would have been no accounting for seasonal weather – death can strike at any time of the year!

As most of these kings died in conflict, there must have been some sort of pact, an unwritten law, which allowed decent passage for the dead *en route* to Iona. How else could the body of a defeated king be transported while a victorious army was in control of the surrounding countryside?

An interesting wee point to finish on here is that of Creag na Marbh, the Rock of the Dead, which stands on Loch Feochan, a few miles south of Oban. This is a natural jetty formed from the rock on the loch shore. It was from here that the galleys would set sail with their royal charge on his final journey. It stands a mile or so north of the village of Kilninver.

Part II: Elsewhere

Dunfermline Abbey seemed to succeed Iona as the royal sepulchre of Scotland. **Malcolm Canmore** was killed in battle and was originally buried near where he fell at Tynemouth in northern England in 1093. He was later transferred to Dunfermline. Malcolm Canmore's wife was later canonised and became **St Margaret**. She was also interred in Dunfermline. They were later buried together in a richly decorated shrine at the eastern end of the abbey in 1250. The remains of this shrine can still be seen just outwith the walls of the abbey.

Malcolm and Margaret are no longer at Dunfermline, however. Margaret's head was kept in a silver case, and was a much-venerated relic. In 1560 it is mentioned as being at Edinburgh Castle by request of Mary Queen of Scots, in 1567 it was in keeping at the Laird of Durie's house, in 1597 the Jesuits took receipt of it, in 1620 it was on show in Antwerp, then in 1627 it was taken to the Scots College at Douay, where it was reported that the strawberry-blond hair was still visible on the head, but the relic disappeared at the time of the French Revolution.

The rest of Margaret's body, along with that of Malcolm, was taken by a Spanish ship that sailed up the Firth of Forth at the time of the Reformation in Scotland, supposedly for safe keeping from reforming zeal. Their remains are now kept at the church of St Lawrence at the Escorial in Madrid. Strange that an early medieval Scots king and queen should end up in such a place. I feel that any remains should be returned to Scotland, the land that they ruled over. It seems only fitting.

Between them, Malcolm and Margaret had six sons, three of whom became Kings of Scots. All are buried at Dunfermline. Edward, Edmund and Ethelred never acceded to the crown. **King Edgar** died in 1107. He was succeeded by his brother **Alexander** I, who reigned from 1107 to 1124. He died in Stirling Castle and was buried in Dunfermline alongside his queen, **Sibylla**.

David I is well remembered for his passion for church-building. He was also buried here, along with his two queens. His son Malcolm IV, better known in our history books as

The remains of a Roman bath-house in Strathclyde Park near Motherwell and close to the M74 motorway – evidence of the attempted Roman occupation of Scotland. A Roman camp stood on the rise in the background.

St Margaret's shrine at the east end of Dunfermline Abbey.
The bodies of St Margaret and Malcolm Canmore once rested here but were
removed during the Reformation and taken to the Escorial in Madrid.

The rebuilt tomb of Princess Marjory, daughter of Robert the Bruce and 'mother' of the Stewart dynasty due to her marriage to Bruce's High Steward. It stands in Paisley Abbey.

The tomb of King Robert the Bruce in Dunfermline Abbey.
Many of Scotland's royals are buried here but this is the only one marked today.

A cast of the skull of Robert the Bruce that sits within a case in Dunfermline Abbey. It shows evidence of serious wounds, including a smashed, then healed, orbit round one eye. The two crossed bottom teeth let us see a little of the Bruce that his peers would have recognised.

A little-known monument to Robert the Bruce, at Coillebhrochain, near Pitlochry.

The Moot Hill at Scone where the kings of Scots were crowned. The Stone of Destiny stood here, and a copy now stands, just to the left of the doorway, for visitors to have a 'wee sit on'. Robert II is buried in this vicinity.

The ancient west front of Dunfermline Abbey, looking from Pittencrief Glen.
This building has seen the burial ceremonies of many of Scotland's royals.

The tomb of Robert III in Paisley Abbey.
He died in Rothesay Castle

The pillar at the site of the Carthusian Monastery in Perth, where James I, among others, is buried. He was slain in the Blackfriars Monastery elsewhere in the city.

Malcolm the Maiden, died at the age of twenty-four in the year 1165, and was the last royal to be interred in Dunfermline Abbey for a number of years. So what happened to the magnificent tombs that would have been erected over these last resting places? We know that Edward Longshanks burnt Dunfermline, and this would have destroyed much of the ornate work, and while some stonework must have survived, it seems the Reformation dealt with what did survive. And where in the church buildings today do all these personages lie? It would seem most are under the little northern projection of the abbey where the gift shop is located today. It is a pity that the building looks so austere. Wouldn't it be wonderful to have seen these tombs in all their magnificence, and think how much more we would know of our earlier days in Scotland if all that workmanship had survived? I do feel the weight of ages in Dunfermline, however, and any knowledge helps to categorise it all in my mind's eye.

Next to succeed to the throne of Scotland was Malcolm the Maiden's brother, William I. He reigned from 1165 to 1214 – quite a long period by the standards of the age, and he is probably better known by his nickname William the Lion. He died in Stirling Castle. William was responsible for the building of the great Abbey of Arbroath, and when restoration work was being undertaken on that venerable pile in 1816, his tomb, carved from hewn freestone, was discovered, lying before the church's high altar. A stone plaque marks the spot today, so William at least has a last resting place that can be visited.

William's wife, Ermengarde, was an illegitimate grand-daughter of Henry I of England, and it is said that this was a marriage forced upon him by the English. It should be no surprise, then, that William lies in Arbroath alone, as Ermengarde is interred in the much-ruined Abbey of Balmerino, on the south shore of the Firth of Tay, on a small road west of Newport-on-Tay. William and Ermengarde did manage to produce an heir, though, and Alexander II of Scotland ruled from 1214 to 1249.

Alexander had assembled a fleet prior to quelling insurrection in the Hebrides. The fleet was assembled in Horse-shoe Bay on the Island of Kerrera off Oban when Alexander suddenly took ill.

He was carried ashore and died in a pavilion erected on a spot still called Dalrigh (Gaelic for 'King's Field'). The surprising thing in all this is that Alexander's body was transported right across Scotland to be buried at Melrose Abbey in the Borders. Some of the journey may have been done by water, of course, perhaps his fleet sailing to the Firth of Clyde, but Alexander II did have connections with Melrose and must have left instructions that he wished to be buried there. He was interred by the high altar. A dark-coloured slab of polished limestone has been pointed out as his tombstone, but this is only circumstantial.

He left a son, only eight years of age, who mounted the throne and reigned from 1249 to 1286. **Alexander** – the third of that name. It was this Alexander whose horse lost its footing and fell over the cliffs at Kinghorn, leaving Scotland in a turmoil that was to lead to the Wars of Independence. A monument at the roadside marks the spot where his body was found. A local brewery makes a particularly strong beer named Alexander's Downfall, and the label shows him falling over the cliff!

Alexander, like several of his ancestors, was buried in Dunfermline Abbey, alongside his first wife and his two sons, David and Alexander, who predeceased him, and there is nothing today to mark their last resting place.

Alexander's daughter had married the King of Norway, but died in childbirth, and so the next in line to the throne of Scotland was his little granddaughter, Margaret, who is better known as **The Maid of Norway**. She was queen in name only, as she died in Orkney aged only seven before she could reign over her kingdom. Her body was taken back to Norway and she was buried in Bergen Cathedral. This cathedral is long gone, but a pillar stands on the site, listing the names of those who have been buried there. The list includes both the Maid and her mother.

After the Maid's death, Edward Longshanks of England acted as arbitor to the many claimants of the Scots crown. He chose **John Balliol**. He did, after all, have the best claim, being nearest in blood line to the Royal House. Balliol ruled from 1292 to 1296, and was ousted to spend the rest of his life in exile on his family lands in France. He died at his castle of Bailleul en Somme in 1314, and records show that he was buried in the church of St

Waast in Bailleul. Scant remains and earthworks of his castle still exist in woodland outside the village. John Balliol's son **Edward** was crowned as a puppet King of Scots, with English aid during the reign of David II, to act as an English rival to David. His last resting place is not on record, but he may be buried in the church of St Waast like his father.

Next on the list is the mighty Robert I, **the Bruce**, the hero-king of Scots. Bruce reigned from 1306 to 1329, and died at his house of Cardross, on the River Leven, a little north of Dumbarton (nothing to do with the town of Cardross on the Clyde). His body was transported across Scotland to be buried at Dunfermline Abbey. It rested at Dunipace and Cambuskenneth *en route*. Bruce's tomb was rediscovered during the early 1800s, and today is marked by a bronze plaque. It is the only tomb there that can be visited with any certainty today.

Bruce's wife **Elizabeth** is also buried at Dunfermline, although she died at Cullen in Banffshire. Her bowels were removed before her journey south, and were buried at the old kirk in Cullen. Bruce's daughter **Matilda** was also buried at Dunfermline. His eldest daughter, **Marjorie**, married his High Steward, **Walter**. The corruption of Steward to Stewart gave rise to Scotland's famous Stewart dynasty. Both Walter and Marjorie are buried in Paisley Abbey.

Bruce and his queen did produce a son, who in 1329 ascended the throne as **David II**. Unfortunately, he had none of the attributes of his brilliant father, and died in February 1371 in Edinburgh Castle. He became the first royal to be buried in Edinburgh's Holyrood Abbey, which had been built by his ancestor David I.

Holyrood was constructed to house Scotland's other great talisman – the Holy Rood. *Rood* is the old Scots for a cross. This object, in an ornate case, was believed to be a piece of the 'True Cross' on which Christ suffered. It had been brought to Scotland by St Margaret from Hungary. Strangely, Arthur of the Britons was meant to own a piece of the cross, and his descendant Edmund Ironside fled to Hungary – whence Margaret came. Perhaps these pieces were one and the same. David II lost the Holy Rood at the Battle of Neville's Cross, and the English had it displayed at Durham Cathedral, where it supposedly disappeared at the Reformation. Another huge loss.

David II was followed by his nephew, **Robert II**, the first of the Stewart kings. He ruled from 1371 to 1390, and died at Dundonald Castle in Ayrshire. The castle is in a tolerable state of repair and is well worth a visit.

Finding Robert II's last resting place was a real problem for me for quite a time. Some books claimed he was interred in Paisley Abbey. I had seen evidence that his mother and son were there, but I had found no evidence for him, so I was dubious. I think some had assumed he was there perhaps because of its relative proximity to Dundonald.

Strangely, it was a book on Paisley Abbey that I bought in a second-hand shop that finally gave me that piece of the jigsaw. The Reverend Howell's 1929 book charting the history of the Abbey stated, 'Robert II, the first Stewart King, is buried at Scone, but his two wives, Elizabeth Mure and Euphemia Ross, are interred in the Abbey of Paisley.' Once I knew he was buried at Scone it was easy to check and find other scant details to ascertain that Scone was indeed the place. The church at Scone was destroyed at the Reformation, but it is a shame that a King of Scots is buried in the grounds of the later Scone Palace and no mention or marker announces the fact.

His son, **Robert III**, then ruled from 1390 to 1406. He died in Rothesay Castle, and was taken to the mainland to be buried in Paisley Abbey. Queen Victoria commissioned the tombstone of Sicilian marble which marks his tomb today. It was unveiled in 1888.

I remember once on a visit to the abbey of Paisley I was looking at Marjorie Bruce's tomb, and turned to find my daughter, who was about six at the time, walking across the tombstone of Robert III. Of course, she was oblivious to her actions, but I found it strange that a little girl could clamber about on the tomb of a man who, in his day, had the power of life and death over his people. On reflection, I could never imagine the same thing happening at Westminster Abbey without much uproar! Perhaps we do have the best of it. I can imagine that most Scots treated their royalty with the same disdain with which they treat most people who they feel have perhaps got above their station. No bowing and scraping to their majesties here! We are a' Jock Tamson's bairns, as Burns said.

Robert III's eldest son and heir, **David, Duke of Rothesay**, met his end at the hands of assassins and was buried in Lindores Abbey, whose ruins stand in the town of the same name in Fife. The tomb of his daughter **Princess Margaret** survives in the ruins of Lincluden College in Dumfries. Next up for kingship was his younger son, who became **James I**. He reigned from 1406 to 1437. James was murdered in a sewer under the Blackfriars monastery in Perth, where he had tried to escape his attackers. This was also the scene of the incident where Kate Douglas, one of the Queen of Scots' ladies-in-waiting, thrust her arms into the staples for the missing door bar, to try and gain some time for her monarch to escape. This meant that her arms were smashed when the attackers burst into the room, and so she became known to the Scots as Kate Bar-lass. There are still families in the Perth area named Barlas and they proudly claim descent from Kate. Blackfriars is long gone but a plaque in Perth marks the spot. The plaque is on a wall in Blackfriars Street where it meets Charlotte Street. Strangely, James was buried within a different Perth monastery, the Carthusian, a building for which he seemed to have a special liking. Although it too is long gone, its site is marked with a pillar, at the junction of King Street and County Place, in front of the King James VI Hospital buildings. His queen, **Joan Beaufort**, was later buried beside her husband.

The Stewarts were generally an unlucky lot, and **James II** was no exception. He reigned from 1437 to 1460 and was killed by an exploding cannon at the siege of Roxburgh Castle near Kelso. A thorn tree in the grounds of Floors Castle is said to mark the spot. James was taken to Edinburgh and was buried in Holyrood Abbey. His queen, **Mary of Gueldres**, was buried in the old Trinity College Church in Edinburgh, a building she founded in 1462. This edifice was swept away to make way for Waverley Station in 1848, and her remains were transferred to the new vault in Holyrood Abbey – so she rejoined her husband almost four hundred years after the fact! **James III** reigned from 1460 to 1488, and was slain after the

Battle of Sauchieburn, legend stating that his murder took place at Beatons Mill, a building alongside the Bannock Burn at Milton. This building survived till 1954 when it was destroyed by fire, but the path down to the Bannock here bears a plaque marking the site of the mill. He was interred at the high altar of Cambuskenneth Abbey, not too far away on the north bank of the Forth. A dig in 1864 revealed the tomb of James III and his wife **Margaret of Denmark**, both buried under a large slab of limestone, James in an oak coffin. A cast was made of James's skull for a local museum, but this now unfortunately cannot be traced. Their remains were re-interred in an oak box, and a new stone memorial was erected over them in 1865, by the orders of Queen Victoria.

Cambuskenneth is open to the public, and James and Margaret's tomb stands surrounded by railings amidst the venerable ruins. **James IV** then ruled from 1488 till 1513. James was a good king – impetuous but beloved by the people of Scotland.

He died in battle, along with many thousands of his subjects, on Flodden Field. His corpse was found the next day among a pile of dead. A hand hung by a strip of skin, his neck cut and his body full of arrows. His body was taken to Berwick, was disemboweled and embalmed and sent on to London. It eventually ended up in Sheen Monastery in Surrey – now long gone. John Stow, chronicler of London in those times, saw the body, and said that workmen cut off the head. Elizabeth I's master glazier, Lancelot Young, took the head home to his London house, but it was eventually buried in St Michael's Church in London's Wood Street in an unmarked grave along with English bones that had been cleared from the crypt of the church.

The fate of the rest of the body is unknown. Strangely, St Michael's was demolished in the early 1900s, and the ground is now owned by Standard Life of Edinburgh. At time of writing, archaeological work is being carried out on the site, and the possibility of marking the site with a plaque to James IV is under discussion.

James IV's wife, **Margaret Tudor**, is buried at the site of the Carthusian monastery in Perth where lie James I and his queen. Legend says that James first married **Margaret Drummond**, daughter of Lord Drummond, and that she was poisoned along with her two sisters by jealous nobles eager for the advancement of the dynastic marriage with the English princess. Margaret Drummond and her sisters were buried in Dunblane Abbey and the three slabs in the floor of the abbey are marked as their tombs. James IV left a son, yet another James, and he ruled from 1513 to 1542.

James V died just after hearing the news of the defeat of the Scots at the Battle of Solway Moss. He was staying at Falkland Palace and basically turned his face to the wall and gave up on life. He was only thirty-one. His body was taken to Holyrood Abbey in Edinburgh for burial. His first wife, **Magdalen**, was also buried here.

I'm sure you will be interested in the following passage, which comes from a manuscript of Sir Robert Sibbalds, which is preserved in the Advocates' Library. The following devastation took place in Holyrood by a mob, fired up because James VII had celebrated mass within.

I have translated it into modern language simply to make it more accessible:

Upon the 24th of January 1683, by procurement of the Bishop of Dunblane, I went into a vault on the south-east corner of the abbey church of Holyrood, and there were present the Lord Strathnaver and the Earl of Forfar, Mr Robert Scott, Minister of the Abbey, the Bishop of Dunblane, and several others.

We viewed the body of King James V of Scotland. It lay within a wooden coffin and is covered with a leaden coffin. There seemed to be hair upon the head still. The body was two lengths of my staff, and two inches more, that is, two inches and more above two Scots elns, for I measured the staff with an elnwand afterwards. The body was coloured black with the balsam that preserved it, which was like melted pitch. The Earl of Forfar took the measure with his staff likewise.

There were plates of lead, in several long pieces, loose upon and about the coffin, which carried the following inscription, as I take it from before the Bishop and Noblemen in the aisle of the said church, *Illustris Scotorum Rex Jacobus, ejus nom. v . . .*

Next to the south wall in a smaller niche lay a short coffin, with the teeth still in the skull. To this little coffin seemed to belong the inscription, made out of long plates of lead in the Saxon character, *Magdalena Francisii Regi Franciae Primaginita Regina Scotorum, Sponsa de Jacobi v.*

Arnots' notes on Holyrood in his book on Edinburgh stated:

> In AD 1776 we had seen the body of James V and some others in their leaden coffins. These coffins were now stolen. The head of Queen Magdalen, which was then entire and even beautiful, and the skull of Darnley [Mary Queen of Scots' husband] were also stolen. His thigh bones, however, still remain, and are proof of the vastness of his stature.

Astonishing stuff, and there is more to come. James V was succeeded by his little daughter **Mary**, Queen of Scots, the only queen to reign over Scotland in her own right and not as a queen consort.

As a child I was familiar with the rhyme 'Mary Queen of Scots got her head chopped off!' and for some reason we used to pull the heads off dandelions as we were saying this. Mary reigned from 1542 to 1567.

Her first husband was the Dauphin of France. When she returned to Scotland she was first married to **Darnley**. He died at Kirk O' Field in Edinburgh in 1567, a mystery that has intrigued for many years, foul play obviously involved. He was buried in Holyrood Abbey, and Sibbalds reported after the destruction caused by James VII's mass.

> Upon the south side, next to the King's body [James V], lay one great coffin of lead with a body in it. The muscles of the thigh seemed to be entire, and the balsam stagnating in some quantity at the foot of the coffin. There appeared no inscription upon the coffin, but it was most likely King Henry Darnley's.

Mary's next husband was **Bothwell**. He eventually fled to Denmark where he was arrested for an earlier misdemeanour.

Bothwell spent the last eleven years of his life in horrific captivity. He died chained to a pillar so he could not stand upright, driven mad by his ill treatment, with matted hair and covered in filth, in the prison of Dragsholm. His mummified body is still on show in Faarevejle church near the prison. Mary was beheaded in Fotheringhay Castle – it took the drunken axeman three strokes to dispatch her. She was first buried at Peterborough Cathedral, where a plaque to her memory stands. She was later transferred to Westminster Abbey in London, where a marvellous white marble effigy of her adorns her tomb. On my last visit to Westminster I noticed a sign by her tomb which stated that she had been 'beheaded for treason'. I was outraged. How can a monarch be accused of treason? Especially a monarch of Scotland being accused of treason against another nation. Injustices like this do not impress me, and demonstrate to me the arrogance of others.

Mary was followed by her son **James VI** of Scotland, who reigned from 1567 to 1603, then when he inherited the throne of England he ruled Great Britain until 1625. He was buried in Westminster Abbey. So ends the story of the burial places of the line of Scotland.

Succeeding monarchs are styled as rulers of 'Great Britain', although as many Scots have an interest in Jacobite affairs, they may be interested to know that **James VII** is buried in Paris, in a marble tomb in the suburb of Saint Germain en Laye and both the **'Old Pretender'** and his son, **Bonnie Prince Charlie**, are in the Vatican, where their tombs can be visited.

I hope that some of this information will help you to find the landscape of Scotland even more colourful than before. I have had some good times putting it all together!

The Insignia

The Thistle

There are certain symbols we all see as being particularly Scottish, and obviously these things have histories of their own.

Take the thistle, for instance. Why is the thistle the plant we think of when we are looking for something that represents the flora of our nation?

It is a strange wee story, but all the sources seem to tally on this one.

Apparently, many centuries ago, an army of Scots was sleeping in some woodland. An army of Vikings discovered that they were there and, to try and sneak up on them and take them unawares, the Vikings removed their boots so that they would make no noise. Unfortunately for the Vikings, they walked through a patch of forest where thistles were growing prodigiously, and they stood on them, letting out yelps which alerted the Scots to their presence, and the attack was thwarted. So runs the story – and the Scots since that time have sported the thistle in remembrance of the deed.

It is such a bizarre little story and so widely known in Scotland that it must have some element of truth in it.

Other than that, of course, thistles grow liberally all over the landscape of Scotland.

The Lion Rampant

On to the Lion Rampant. A clawing lion, raised on its hind legs, and depicted in red, on a background of gold or yellow. All Scots identify with it, although it is the banner of the sovereign or his representative.

The royal badge of Scotland was originally the wild boar. The very same as is carved into the living rock of Dunadd, where the Scots first landed. This symbol lasted until the days of King William I, or The Lion, as he came to be known.

William reigned around the time of the Crusades. It is possible someone purchased lions at this time and brought them to Scotland, and either gifted or sold them to the King of Scots. We can imagine people in Scotland seeing lions for the first time. 'Christ Almighty – look at the size of they dogs!'

William was especially fond of Stirling Castle, and part of the castle today is still known as the Lion's Den. This is where the royal lions were originally kept. William was so taken with the King of Beasts that he changed the symbol of Scots royalty from the wild boar to the lion rampant. The symbol he chose is the same as that used to this day.

It is a pity that William did not have the same powerful qualities as his nickname 'The Lion'. He was not as effective a king as his name might suggest.

The Lion Rampant would be carried on the battlefield from this time on, to signify the King of Scots' position.

In 1297, when Wallace was fighting at Stirling Bridge, he left his friend Scrymgeour in charge of the taking of Dundee Castle. This Scrymgeour successfully took the castle and Wallace conferred on him the title Hereditary Standard-Bearer of the King of Scots. Unfortunately, Scrymgeour was captured by the English and suffered the same hideous death as Wallace himself – hanging, drawing and quartering. But he had a son, and that son carried the Lion Rampant banner behind Bruce on the field of Bannockburn. Bruce ratified the hereditary standard-bearer bit, and to this day Scrymgeour has the right to carry the Lion Rampant banner at not only official events but also if the army of Scotland went into battle. Round about 1999 I was at an event in Stirling, and was kilted up. I nodded to another kilted gentleman at the other side of the hall. As fate would have it we were eventually thrown together. 'What do you do?', he asked. I replied that I did a bit of writing, and that my Sunday name was David R Ross. 'What's your name?', I asked.

'Murray Scrymgeour.'

'Not the . . . ?'

But he was. I looked at his face and wondered if this was a face Wallace would have recognised. We chatted. He spoke about Wallace as if he last talked to him on Saturday. I just thought to myself, 'How can this guy sleep at night with that blood line?' I would be turning all those thoughts of the past over in my mind, but, of course, he was just who he was. He told me what generation he was since Wallace had conferred the title of Standard-Bearer on his ancestor. Twenty-something down the line, father to son.

Good God – I don't even know who my great grandfather was!

The Crown Jewels

The Crown jewels of Scotland (or, as they are better known, The Honours) are kept within Edinburgh Castle, where the Stone of Destiny now resides.

The crown, sceptre and sword of state are, I believe, the oldest Crown jewels in the world. Certainly they are older than their English equivalents.

The crown was remodelled in 1540 and is said to contain the gold from the circlet worn by Robert the Bruce. Certainly all the gold used in the crown originated in Scotland. It is set with ninety-four pearls, ten diamonds and thirty-three other gems. The sword of state was a gift from Pope Julius II to James IV, and was made in Italy.

The crown, sword and sceptre have been joined over the years by other regalia: the Lord Treasurer's rod, the George (a type of medallion) of James V, the collar of the Garter that belonged to James VI, and the St Andrew and coronation ring that belonged to Charles I.

The crown, sword and sceptre have seen some adventures in their day. They were taken to Dunnottar Castle, just south of Stonehaven, in 1651, as it was thought this cliff-girt fortress would be the safest place to keep them during this time, as English troops had overrun Scotland during Cromwell's campaign. Cromwell's troops besieged the castle, which was under the command of George Ogilvy of Barras. Ogilvy eventually had to surrender due to starvation, but prior to this a stratagem was used to smuggle the regalia out of Dunnottar. Mrs Granger, wife of the minister of nearby Kinneff, asked permission to visit Ogilvy's wife within the castle. Permission was granted, and she, while within, hid the crown in her clothing and wrapped the sword and sceptre in lint which she carried. When she emerged, the English general actually helped her onto her horse, and she kept her cool admirably. That night, her husband, the minister, buried the regalia under the flagstones of his church. There they remained until 1660, when George Ogilvy, the custodian of Dunnottar, presented them to Charles II. Ogilvy was created a baronet, but poor Granger and his wife received no reward for all the risk they had undertaken. There is a monument to Mrs Granger at the church, though.

At the time of the Union between Scotland and England in 1707, the Crown jewels were lodged in Edinburgh Castle. Part of the Treaty of Union stated that they would always be kept in Scotland, but the populace began to believe that they had been conveyed by stealth to London, as they had not been seen for years. So many articles of the Treaty had been broken or ignored, it was only when a commission searched the castle in 1818, headed by Sir Walter Scott, that they were found, forgotten and neglected in an old oak chest. Since that time The Honours have always been open to the view of the public.

The Flag of Scotland

So, on to the flag of Scotland, the white St Andrew's cross on a sky-blue background. This is more than a flag – it is the picture of an event. It is also the oldest flag in the world, and it is surprising how few Scots realise that this is the case.

An army of Picts and Scots were being pursued through East Lothian by an English army, led by their king, Athelstan. The Scots, realising that they would probably be cut to ribbons, decided to make a stand and at least die fighting like men. They crossed a ford and lined up in battle-order on the far side. As they awaited the appearance of their foes, a large white cross, the cross of St Andrew, appeared in the blue summer sky. They realised that God had given them a sign, and boldly met their enemies as they crossed the ford. They pressed the English hard, eventually causing great slaughter, and their king was also slain, Athelstan falling among many of his people. The Scots and Picts, very soon to be united as one nation, adopted what they had seen and turned it into their banner, their symbol, the flag of every one of them. The white cross on a background the colour of the summer sky. It has been the symbol of Scotland for well over a thousand years.

The village that stands on the battle site today has taken its name from the fight. Athelstaneford. The church in the village dates back to *c*.1100 in its original form. There is a memorial to the battle in the churchyard in the shape of a standing stone, showing the armies fighting with the cross stretching across the sky behind them.

It should be explained that when St Andrew was crucified, he said that he was not worthy to be martyred in the same way as his master, Jesus, therefore he was crucified on an x-shaped cross. There has been debate about the date of the battle; I have seen claims for a date as early as 736AD, but it is generally believed to have been 832AD.

So the flag of Scotland is a representation of the sky that day. Every kid in Scotland should know the story. Every time I see the Saltire (the name we affectionately call our flag) it sums up my whole nation and all its history.

Wallace's men knew it – it flew at Stirling Bridge. Bruce's men knew it – it flew at Bannockburn. It has gone wherever Scots have gone, the world over. And I feel it is a flag of friendship, too. When in the USA or Canada, I see expats flying it from their houses, or it flies from a flagpole in their garden. It doesn't bother anyone, nobody sees it as inflammatory in any way. People the world over do not see it as a flag of oppression, and that is something to be proud of. I am always happy to see it stuck on cars. I identify with it. It makes me proud. My only desire now is to see it fly outside the European Parliament or the United Nations. We may have the oldest flag in the world, but we are not seriously recognised, and another flag flies in its place to represent us.

Recently, in an antique shop in Edinburgh, I mentioned to the guy behind the counter how much things have changed in my lifetime. As a kid, getting taken to Edinburgh was a big day out. My mum had a feel for history and used to like to wander the city absorbing the atmosphere. The buildings mostly flew Union Jacks and I always remember emerging from Waverley Station and seeing the big one that flew atop the North British Hotel. The North British (a horrific term for a nation as old as ours) is now the Balmoral, and flies a big Saltire. In fact, nearly every building in the city centre flies a Saltire. I feel the change.

Mentioning this in the shop, the assistant turned and replied, 'One day we will have the Saltire flying above Edinburgh Castle and I'll know that our time has come.'

Edinburgh Castle flies the Union Jack as it is a garrison of the British Army. When the flag of Scotland flies above it proudly once more, we will indeed know our time has come. Our eyes met as he said this and I knew I had met a kindred spirit. This thought had often crossed my mind, but I was surprised that someone else mentioned it without prompting.

One day I will come out of Waverley Station, or drive along Princes Street on my motorbike, and glance up at the castle as I always do, and one day the flag of Scotland will be flying there.

And if a tear does not come, I'll be surprised. It is a symbol that I have waited my whole life to see.

Wallace and Bruce

WHAT MAKES A SCOT? Why does the person next to me regard himself as being Scottish? What do they have in common with me? It is more than sharing a country, more than being part of the same nation. As an expat Scot is not staying in Scotland but still feels its pull, it is the shared history that matters. Their ancestors went through the same turmoil as mine. They fought the same enemies, in the same battles, and underwent the same upheavals through the centuries. The common culture matters. A nation is the result of its history. If that history is destroyed or demeaned, it undermines the whole fabric of the country. The destruction of the history of nations still takes place, in an attempt to exterminate a nation's peculiar nationalism. The Soviet Union did it in such places as Armenia, and China has imposed its own brand of history on its neighbours. At school I heard very little that concerned Scotland's history, and what there was was often blurred by the 'British' contribution.

I discovered Scotland's history by accident, discovering first the novels of Nigel Tranter, moving on to people like John Prebble, then reading as many academic history books as I could lay my hands on. I am particularly indebted to GWS Barrow of Edinburgh University, an Englishman no less, whose work on Robert the Bruce is the bible of the days of Wallace and Bruce, and goes a long way to uncovering the facts and giving us an understanding of those times.

Every country has its heroes. Scotland has many, but the two foremost are Wallace and Bruce. Wallace, the man with the common touch, started the fight and paid the ultimate penalty for his beliefs. Bruce, of royal blood, won the victory, and died in his bed, worn out from the rigours of his life – but it was a life lived to the full. They, between them, very much shaped the psyche of Scotland as it is today. I don't live in the past, incidentally, but we have to learn from what has gone before. We, like all peoples, need to learn from our past.

These people lived seven hundred years ago, and I suppose

seven hundred years seems an absolute eternity to many. Wallace must seem like ancient history. I remember listening to a talk on Wallace where the speaker mentioned that he lived twenty-five generations ago. That is roughly the case, but I began to think of the late Nigel Tranter, who wrote so succinctly about Wallace and Bruce, and Nigel lived into his nineties. By his timescale, Wallace and Bruce lived only eight of his lifetimes ago. It's not really that far back in time, is it?

When my book *On the Trail of William Wallace* was published, it went to number nine in the Scottish book charts in its first week. I should state that no one was more surprised than me – I was, after all, a complete unknown. Suddenly I was doing slide shows and talks on Wallace all over Scotland. Sometimes I felt out of my depth, or felt I had bitten off more than I could chew. One night, driving north from East Kilbride where I stay, I remember glancing over towards the Wallace Monument atop the Abbey Craig, the light in its crown shining like a beacon. The reality of William Wallace the man suddenly hit me: everything he had undergone; nights spent cold under the stars; the longing for the loved ones he had lost; times when he must have analysed his situation and wondered if he had chosen the correct course for his life; times of despair; times of grim satisfaction when he achieved what had seemed impossible. This was a flesh and blood man, not just a legend, not just the subject of a Hollywood film. Once upon a time people looked upon him, and he was there. He could open his mouth and announce 'I am William Wallace'.

I realised that what I did, getting up in front of people and saying a few words, was, in reality, very little.

Like Wallace, I have tried to do my best for Scotland. I have had people say that I am like a modern Wallace, but all I can say to that is that I am not fit to lace the boots of William Wallace.

He gave all. I just tell the story.

I have spent much of my life finding the sites associated with Wallace, and many of them I have visited over and over again. Places I can't help but stop at if I am driving in their vicinity. They can have a different feel from one day to the next, from rain to shine, from summer to winter. The landscape of Scotland has not changed in thousands of years. Most folk probably don't give it a thought, but the Scotland we know is the Scotland Wallace knew. We may live in a technological age, but the hills and rivers are still as he knew them. The Sidlaws are just as they were. The Campsies haven't moved much. The Ochils rise up out of the flood plains of the Forth as they did on the day of the Battle of Stirling Bridge.

I wonder what Wallace would think of someone like me who has made a bit of a hobby out of visiting places associated with his life? I imagine he would be really surprised to know that seven hundred years on people would care. I can stand at the memorial in Smithfield, London, on the site of his horrific murder, and think how it must have been for him on the day.

The horror of it all. The degradation. And all these years on people still care.

Every time I visit there are flowers left at the monument's base or tied to the railings in front. I'm sure no one would be more shocked than William Wallace himself. As far as he was concerned, he was doing his best for his people and his country, both of which he loved dearly.

All I can say is he must have been a hell of a man to be remembered so passionately after all this time. And not just in this time. William Wallace will be remembered by Scots till the end of time.

What would Scotland be today if Wallace had never existed? He is the father of our patriotism. He is the memory we turn to when times are hard. If he had never been would Scotland be a distant memory?

Wallace is the figurehead, but so many of his compatriots died for the same beliefs: Andrew Murray, his co-commander at Stirling Bridge; Sir Simon Fraser, whose head was eventually spiked next to Wallace's on London Bridge; Alexander Scrymgeour, his standard-bearer, torn to pieces at Newcastle; Sir John the Graham, and Sir John Stewart, killed at Falkirk; and what of the legendary names recorded by his later biographer, Blind Harry? People like Stephen of Ireland, portrayed brilliantly in *Braveheart*, and Kerlie, who died at Wallace's capture at Robroyston near Glasgow, trying to protect his master. These make up only the tip of the iceberg. Thousands of Scots died fighting the cause that Wallace believed in. They may have thought that theirs was a lost cause at time of death, but they have each and every one shaped the Scotland we know today.

In recent years we have discovered more about the real William Wallace. The rediscovery of the Lubeck letter, one of many sent to European ports after Stirling Bridge, saying that Scotland was free to trade again, was an important step. The seal was intact, and it bore the words *William filius Alan* – William son of Alan. William Wallace's father's name was always in doubt, most old histories giving it as Malcolm, but the truth is now known.

We have a pretty accurate idea of the origins of his family, too. It is believed the Wallaces came north from the Welsh Marches at the time of David I of Scotland. They originated from a village called Ness in Shropshire, close to the Welsh border. Great Ness and Little Ness can still be found on your average road map. They came north with their feudal superiors, the Fitzalans, who became the Royal Stewards or Stewarts of Scotland, eventually becoming the ruling house. These Stewards or Fitzalans were granted land in the Paisley/Renfrew area, Renfrew being known as 'The Cradle of the Stewarts'. They parcelled out the land to their followers, the Ness family being given Elderslie, West of Paisley. They would say to the locals, 'I'm Adam of Ness' or 'I'm Richard of Ness' but of course Ness meant nothing to the locals, so they would address them as 'the Wallaces' – the old Scots for a Welshman. The name stuck, and several generations on William was born. We believe he was born sometime between 1270 and 1274. As you can perhaps imagine, I have many people contacting me with information regarding Wallace, and one source tells me that Wallace was born on 18 January 1275. That is currently under investigation!

There was an archaeological dig at Elderslie in the late 1990s. I stood and watched with Willie Douglas, the Secretary of the Society of William Wallace, in torrential rain. My heart went out to Derek Alexander (good lad!) and the rest of the guys on the dig in those conditions. But what they uncovered fascinated me. Right on the place where the monument stands today they uncovered a moated, fortified building, which was dated to the mid-1200s. We were looking at the building where Wallace probably first saw the light of day. Shards of pottery and other artefacts were found. The site has since been landscaped, with information boards, and a hedge has been planted showing the outline of the original house.

I have travelled all over Scotland doing my Wallace slide show along with my talks on the great man, and it is often as much a learning process for me as it is about imparting information myself. In Coldstream I learned of 'Wallace's Camp', a knoll that has gained an association with Wallace, perhaps by legend, perhaps because Wallace once camped there, maybe before crossing the border during his invasion of Northern England.

There is a memorial to the site of 'Wallace's Hawthorn' in Hawick, a tree that Wallace is said to have tied his horse to whilst in that vicinity. The list goes on, and I love finding another bit of the jigsaw.

One Wallace snippet that should be brought to attention is that following examinations of the Wallace Sword in the National Wallace Monument, it has been stated that the sword is of a style that was prevalent around 1500 and so is too modern for the time of Wallace. What has been overlooked is an entry in the Lord High Treasurer's accounts for 1505, during the reign of James IV:

> Item, for bynding of ane riding sword, ane rappyer, and binding of Wallas sword with cordis of silk, new hilt and plommet [pommel], new scaubert, new belt to the said sword, cost . . . xxvj s.

The sword was obviously believed then to have been the sword captured with Wallace in 1305, and the changes made to it during the reign of James IV have thrown those examining it in modern times, leading them to date it to 1500. One historian, recognising these details, has referred to this weapon as the 'ghost' of the sword of Wallace. The metalwork of the sword will be original, but the parts mentioned above are replacements from 1505. Being reasonably adept in the use of swords, and owning a copy of the Wallace sword in both size and weight, I have found it to be a pretty unweildy beast when compared with most of the other swords I own. I think the original would have had a much longer hilt, thereby balancing out the length of the blade. The size of the sword is impressive enough to look at today, never mind the fact that the original must have been a good bit longer. The blade is shorter, too, as at some point in the past the blade has been broken and repairs have been made, leaving it a little shorter than before. Mention has been made of this in my Wallace book.

As far as I am concerned, a day when I learn something new is a day that hasn't been wasted. Life would be such a bore if you knew your subject inside out. I hope I have many revelations to come, the bigger the better.

His name is everywhere, scattered over the landscape of Scotland. I just wish he knew that his murder was not a useless act. As he died in front of a baying mob of foreigners at the butchers' yards of Smithfield, without even the sustenance of a friendly face, he must have thought that his life's work had been in vain. I know that his last thoughts would have been of Scotland. Well, William, it's seven hundred years on, and I know you will be surprised by this, but we still care about and remember you.

There have been many times in those last seven hundred years when we could have done with having you or your like around. We could do with having politicians who have your single minded devotion, but at least you left us your memory to bolster us for time to come.

William Wallace has helped me meet some interesting people along the way, people who are intensely proud of Wallace. He has had as much of an influence on their lives as he seems to have had on mine. John and Linda Anderson, who run their 'MacBraveheart' website and have organised Braveheart conventions that people have attended from all over the world; Brendan McCabe and Jim Singer, who help organise the Wallace March from Stonehaven to Dunnottar Castle every year. Legend tells us how Wallace stormed Dunnottar, and one look at the place will make it clear to anyone what a task that must have been! The English garrison, with nowhere to go but over the cliffs, took refuge within the chapel. Wallace fired it, killing them all. There is a wreath-laying ceremony inside this little chapel, which is still complete to the wallhead, every year, and to stand on the spot is poignant and touching.

All the people I meet at the Wallace Days at Elderslie, and at the annual meeting at the monument to his capture at Robroyston near Glasgow, feel what I feel – what Wallace felt about Scotland – as do individuals like Gary Stewart from the William Wallace Tartan Army, and many of his compatriots who announce their patriotism through their love of football.

We have the Andrew Murray Project based in the Black Isle, with a march every year from Avoch to the ruins of Ormonde Castle, to commemorate Wallace's co-commander at Stirling Bridge. Murray was killed in the fight and was buried at nearby Fortrose Cathedral, though there is no memorial to him (something we could possibly remedy). In the centre of Ormonde Castle, on its hill, stands a memorial cairn and flagpole. This cairn was erected by a local, Charlie Beattie, who carried each and every stone to the top to build it. Charlie, I take my hat off to you! He just wanted to do something to show his patriotism, and this was his particular way.

I have always appreciated the Avoch (pronounced Och!) sign as you drive into the village; it depicts a party of Scots raising a Saltire.

And the thing that strikes me again and again is just how nice these people are. This is not an ugly small-minded Anglophobic nationalism. This is a friendly help-anyone-in-trouble patriotism, a pride in Scotland and its past that shines through these individuals.

Perhaps I am biased. Perhaps my view of Wallace is rose-tinted. The English chroniclers hated him for his low-born status, probably the ruling classes in Scotland shared that view. There would have been many in Scotland who loathed and feared Wallace. But he was the man who raised his head when all others in Scotland were down. He died for his beliefs, and as he died he probably would have been unable to envisage Robert the Bruce being crowned king and carrying on the fight only six months later.

Bruce the man has always been the yardstick on which we should measure ourselves, and we would all be found wanting. Yes, he fought for a throne where Wallace fought for Scotland. He had as much of a struggle with trying to unite the Scots as he had with the English. It has always been the Scots themselves who have been their own worst enemies, and it is a failing that has always been part of our make-up. For instance, Walter Bower, the monk who wrote the *Scotichronicon*, a history of Scotland written about 1440, penned a chapter entitled 'Division is the most dangerous thing in a kingdom'. This was a lesson aimed at Scots to get them to stand together. Bower also penned such lines as 'How foolish is Scotland in not being instructed in wisdom! How can you prosper if you always succour dangerous foes who have vowed to oppose you?'

I remember when *Braveheart* was premièred at Stirling in 1995; the news cameras were there in force. One of Scotland's leading politicians was interviewed on leaving the première and was asked what he thought. He replied something along the lines of, 'It was all a long time ago – and anyway, Wallace was a loser!'

I was livid. He just could not see that the film was about sticking together, and how Scotland was let down by her 'leaders' taking the wrong stance and the horror that caused. It was seven hundred years on and he was exactly what the film spoke of and did not even realise it himself. This was a man who was meant to represent Scotland in England, but like so many other 'leaders' he really represented England in Scotland.

Ian Hamilton, the man responsible for the liberation of the Stone of Destiny from Westminster Abbey in 1950, once asked me how I felt as far as Scotland was concerned. I told him I sometimes despaired, and the above is a perfect example.

So this brings us neatly back to Bruce. He managed to overcome the divisions and bring Scotland together as a single unit, uniting the various factions to form a coherent front. Sometimes it was done through bargaining, sometimes through promise of position, sometimes it was done through bloodshed and force of arms, and sometimes through sheer force of personality. This was neatly summed up by the writer Agnes Mure MacKenzie when she wrote: 'Robert the Bruce knew Scotland, knew every class of her people, as no man who ruled here before or since has done. It was he who asked of her a miracle – and she accomplished it.'

This sums up one facet of Bruce. But there were others. He had to withstand the unbearable knowledge that his womenfolk were incarcerated in cages, and that many of his friends were dying hideous deaths because of their adherence to his and

Scotland's cause. His brothers all died at English hands, Edward the only one lucky enough to die in battle, the rest suffering disembowelment and beheading. But he never once wavered from the course of Scotland's freedom. I first read his story as a teenager, in the form of Nigel Tranter's *The Bruce Trilogy* and it seemed unbelievable that one man could have undergone so much pain and success in one lifetime. But he did. At a talk in the Museum of Scotland in Edinburgh recently, one of the academics mentioned Bruce, saying that of all the heroes of the world, past, present and future, he was up there with the best of them – and so he is.

As with Wallace, since the launch of my Bruce book I have been apprised of various sites that have a connection with the man that I had not stumbled across during my wanderings, or even that matched up with any of the stuff connected with Bruce in history books.

One of the best is the plaque to Bruce that is set into a gable wall and chimney, the remains of a demolished cottage. This stands in a field adjacent to woodland, to the south of the B8019, just after it crosses the River Garry, north-west of Pitlochry. This plaque reads:

Coillebhrochain
Robert the Bruce
Rested here after
The Battle of Methven

It is very unlikely that he did, as after Methven Bruce headed west along Lochearnside, then north up Glen Ogle and over to Dochart. It is possible he was here on a later campaign, however, and the story of his visit has remained – just the time was wrong. However, it's nice to find that someone, somewhere, sometime, has cared enough (and spent the money) to commemorate Bruce in some way.

A plaque was recently unveiled in Dumbarton at the remains of the church where legend states Bruce's viscera were buried before his final journey across Scotland to his tomb in Dunfermline. The plaque reads that Bruce's heart was carried on crusade by 'A Knight Templar'. Where do these stories come from? I'm happy that the plaque exists, but why deliberately misinform? The Good Sir James, the Black Douglas, carried Bruce's heart – why describe him as a Knight Templar? There is no documentation anywhere that states that this was the case. And talking of Templars, some of the stories that have originated around Roslin Chapel are ludicrous indeed. Jesus's head is under a pillar, for one. All I can say to the people who write the books that contain these 'facts' is – show us. As simple as that. Stop peddling personal theories. Just show us the reality, or show us the documentation. Where is the truth in this? I've always been interested in the legends surrounding Wallace and Bruce and how they have been perceived over the centuries, but personal theories should be portrayed just as that – theories and not the absolute truth.

Roslin Chapel has one Bruce connection that at least deserves an airing. There is a carven face within the chapel that is said to be a representation of the death mask of Bruce. It was supposed to be just a story, but then some interesting facts were brought to my attention. I was doing a talk and slide show on Bruce in a museum in Biggar when Dr McLeod from the Royal Infirmary of Edinburgh introduced himself. He worked at the Dental Institute. He had been working on a reconstruction of Bruce's face from a cast of his skull, taken from the opening of his tomb in the early 1800s.

He invited me over to his offices for a look at his work. I have often looked closely at the several casts of Bruce's skull taken from the original, but you see a completely different picture when things are pointed out by someone who knows what they are doing!

He indicated the groove on the brow that had obviously been caused by a blow from a sharp weapon such as a sword. There was another cut on the chin. None of these were fatal, of course, but they would have left nasty scars.

Most revealing, however, was the damage to one of the eye sockets. I can't believe that I never noticed before how badly smashed it is. It is completely misshapen, and must have been caused by an extremely severe blow from a dull object of some sort, perhaps a mace. Although the bone had knitted and healed, I was informed that Bruce would only have had limited vision on one side because of the severity of the damage. All just part of being the hero-king, I suppose. These were hard times, and battle commanders like Bruce must all have sported similar wounds. Probably they were worn with pride. After all, dexterity in arms was what made a man famous in those times – and Scotland certainly needed all the warriors it could muster.

Dr McLeod finished by revealing the rebuilt head of Robert the Bruce. He said he was sure he had it so spot on that if Bruce's close friend, the Good Sir James, walked into the room he would have immediately recognised it as Bruce. I just stood and stared. Not a young and pretty face, but a scarred, haggard one. But, of course, this was not the face of a young Bruce, or even the victor of Bannockburn. This is how Bruce looked at the very end of his life, after years of warfare and hard living.

But it was a face that had a certain *je ne sais quoi*. It was the face of a man who demanded respect. The face of a man who if he walked into a room would have turned every head. It was the face of Robert the Bruce, the hero-king of Scots, and I felt extremely privileged. Some days just stand out, and Dr McLeod gave me one of those days. But he also told me an extraordinary tale. He had compared the skull and his reconstruction with the face carved in Roslin Chapel, and there were, astonishingly, many similarities. The puckered scars were there, the damaged eye socket is very apparent, and the face shape is right. How could this be? The following, I am careful to point out, is personal theory, but I hope it interests and intrigues.

When the Douglas carried Bruce's heart on crusade, one of his companions was William Sinclair of Roslin. Is it possible Douglas had a death mask of Bruce? I can see him sitting in his cabin as his ship crossed the Bay of Biscay, eyeing the casket containing the heart of his late master and friend, and perhaps looking from it to the death mask lying alongside it. Douglas was killed in battle at Teba in Andalusia and we know that his body was brought back to Scotland by the survivors, one of whom was William Sinclair of Roslin. Could Sinclair have brought back the death mask, then at some future point was a mason commissioned to copy this mask into the ornate stonework of Roslin? Theory, of course, but the hard fact remains that the face at Roslin matches very closely that which we know of Bruce.

When my Bruce book was published I toured round Scotland to promote it. One of the events was held in the James Thin bookshop in Dumfries. I was lucky that night as there was a reporter from the *Dumfries and Galloway Standard* in the audience, a man by the name of Doug Archibald. Doug was a patriot, and held Bruce in particular esteem. He introduced himself and spoke to me after the event. He told me a very interesting story and later sent me photocopies of the original reports from the press.

At the tail end of the 1800s, construction work was taking place at the side of Dumfries's Burns Square, the side that stands nearest the River Nith. As this building work was taking place, the workmen uncovered some tombs that were obviously the last resting places of clergymen, this being ascertained from the artefacts discovered within. The proper authorities were called in, and excavations made.

The site of an altar was discovered, and it was realised that this was the remains of the Greyfriars Monastery which had once stood in the town, the building where Bruce had stabbed the Red Comyn before assuming the Crown of Scotland. Bruce did not strike the fatal blow – Kirkpatrick of Closeburn finished off Comyn – but the crime was seen as Bruce's own. It was realised that when news of this act reached the Vatican the Pope would take steps to excommunicate Bruce, so steps had to be taken quickly to have Bruce crowned as an excommunicate would not be able to go through the act of coronation.

As these excavations took place it was discovered that on the opposite side of the altar there were two more tombs, but these were very different from the tombs that contained the bodies of the churchmen. These tombs contained the bodies of what were obviously warriors, armed and clad in armour.

It became clear that these were probably the bodies of Comyn and his uncle. His uncle was present on the day and had leapt to Comyn's defence but was slain in the fracas. Circumstances would have made a hasty burial of the bodies a necessity. Bruce was hardly likely to have contacted Comyn's relatives to arrange collection of the body! There had been trouble between Bruce and Comyn in the past, most notably at a meeting in Peebles where a fight had broken out and daggers were drawn, so there was obviously no love lost between them.

So it seems that we know what became of the Red Comyn, but what has happened since these finds? According to Doug the site was basically left as it was, and a covering of concrete was constructed above the remains. A row of shops now covers the site. It's easy to find, though, as a plaque erected by the Saltire Society is on a connecting wall between two of the shops that stand directly above the remains of the monastery. The other shops have cellars but the ones at the plaque do not, due to the remains underneath.

The deeds which took place here on that fateful day in 1306 changed the whole history of Scotland. Consolidation. Bannockburn. The Declaration of Arbroath. Freedom.

It is strange to watch the shoppers going about their business unaware of what lies beneath their feet.

Like Wallace, Bruce has left behind all over Scotland places associated with his campaigns, as well as in northern England. At one point he had control of England's north, from the River Ribble at Preston in the west to the Humber in the east. Although the English heavily outnumbered the Scots, Bruce's troops, mounted on their Hobins (little ponies, which gave rise to their riders' nickname, Hobelars, and to the children's play horses we call hobby horses), could outride and outmanoeuvre anything sent against them.

One of Bruce's most resounding victories was won deep into England at the Battle of Old Byland, fought on the edge of the Hambleton Hills, east of Thirsk. On my travels I visited this spot and got into a conversation with a lady who told me she was a member of the local history society. I asked her if there were any mementoes of the battle still to be seen. 'What battle?', she replied. I explained to her that a huge battle had been fought on this spot in October 1322. The Scots were led by their king and Edward II of England was almost captured in the rout following the fight. She had never heard of it. I suppose that may be an essential difference between the two nations. The Scots seem to take pleasure in recalling defeats like Flodden, whereas the English seem to ignore theirs completely.

The lady did remark, however, that the battle may be why there was an area nearby that the locals called 'Scotch Corner' (nothing to do with the similarly named place on the trans-Pennine route further north). Intrigued, I asked for directions. As the A170 crosses over the edge of the escarpment of the Hambletons driving east, a little farm road branches off to the right (south). Down this road a track goes off eastwards and leads to 'Scotch Corner'. There is a strange little private chapel here, and Scotch Corner is marked on the Ordnance Survey 1:50,000 Sheet 100. Part of the battle must have taken place here for the name to have stuck. There was an incident when the Highlanders under Bruce's personal command flanked and attacked the English. Perhaps this was the spot where they arrived on the plateau of the hill.

It never ceases to amaze how much more you can learn from actually walking the terrain as well as learning the story from books. I'm actually scared to admit it but I do get a feeling from the terrain. When I was writing my Bruce book I visited all the pertinent battle sites in England. Part of this entailed an exploration of Weardale, where the Scots had again defied an English army in 1327. Where the various confrontations took place has always been open to conjecture. But I can actually feel the right spots in my soul, as if my fellow countrymen have left behind a footprint. Common sense comes into it too, of course – there are places in the landscape that would be an obvious choice for defence or attack, especially where many hundreds would be involved. But I can feel it, too, although don't ask me to explain it as I don't understand it myself – it's just a gut feeling.

But William Wallace and Robert Bruce, can I just thank the two of you very much as you didn't just save my country from serfdom and oblivion seven hundred years ago. You have given me many years of pleasure, just through being able to scour the countryside visiting sites you have an association with. And it seems endless.

I learn of new sites all the time, and there are some that I really look forward to visiting. When Wallace was returning from

Rome he visited the exiled King John Balliol at his castle on the Somme in northern France. I have several reasons for going there in the near future. I want a look at the church where Balliol is buried, I want to see the remains of the castle. I have seen photos, and the well still seems more or less complete along with the earthworks, now surrounded by woodland. But most of all I want to be able to look out over the surrounding countryside, as Wallace did, to see it seven hundred years on. And I want to see how it makes me feel.

Hey There, Jimmy Stewart

PERHAPS ROBERT THE Bruce was too good. I know that might sound a bit strange but, for some odd reason, after his time we thought that we could win any fight going. Bannockburn had such an effect on the psyche of later commanders that they took terrible risks that led to absolute carnage in battle again and again. Robert the Bruce's greatest asset was prudence. He would not risk a single Scot's life if he could help it, only fighting as a last resort.

This is why history is important!

Later generations just did not learn from the past.

There were bright spots, of course. The Battle of Otterburn in 1388. This is the famous battle where the dead man won the fight. An army of Scots, led by the Douglas, a descendant of the Good Sir James, managed to capture the standard of Henry Percy of Northumberland outside the gates of Newcastle. Percy is perhaps better known by his nickname 'Hotspur'.

Douglas informed Hotspur that if he wished to save face and win back his standard, he could try and catch the Scots before they crossed the border. Nothing loath, Hotspur quickly mustered an army and caught the Scots just as they had camped for the night at Otterburn, by an old Roman camp. The Scots intended to cross the border at Carter Bar on their homeward journey. Although it grew dark, battle was joined. The Scots were outnumbered but fought valiantly. Right at the onset of battle Douglas was stabbed to death, some say by an assassin as he donned his armour. His dying words were to instruct his pages to hide his body so that the rest of the Scots would not know he was dead and so lose heart. He was hidden in a bush.

As the night progressed, the moon rose. It lit a scene of carnage and unreality, Scot grappled with Englishman, each fighting furiously, the dead littering the ground. Sir Hugh Montgomery of Eglington outfought Hotspur himself and forced him to yield. Hotspur asked for the honour of proffering his person as a prisoner to the Douglas himself. He was taken to the bush where

Douglas's body was hidden, and told to yield there. Montgomery then took Hotspur prisoner and took him back to Scotland. He was able to demand a huge ransom for Hotspur's return, which was duly paid. Montgomery used this 'poind' money, as it was called, to build himself a handsome fortress. This castle was built on his lands at Eaglesham in Renfrewshire, and was named Polnoon. Some people have claimed fancifully that it was so named as it was a corruption of *poind* from the ransom, but this would seem to be far-fetched. As I stay only a few miles from Eaglesham, I often wondered where this castle was. In East Kilbride, where I stay, there is an old inn. In fact, I believe it is the oldest building in the town that is not a fortified building, and it is named the Montgomery Arms. Eaglesham has an equivalent named the Eglington Arms, both no doubt taking their name from the bold Sir Hugh. I doubt if there is more than a handful of people in the area that know the story of Otterburn and its connections locally, which shows again how most Scots don't really realise the amazing history that surrounds them. I eventually tracked down the scant remains of this castle, standing high above the infant River Cart, the stones of this once proud fortress scattered right down the hillside to the river. I found it simply by riding around the Eaglesham vicinity on the bike and noticing the names of surrounding properties, like a house named 'Castleview' – an obvious clue there. I take delight in scrambling about sites like this, thinking of the history of these places, and I thought of the calibre of the men who fought on both sides in 1388, and of Hotspur's chivalric persona making him fight to protect the honour contained in trying to recapture his banner.

But Otterburn was not the norm. The Scots took some serious defeats in the centuries after Bannockburn. The worst by far was Flodden. Falkirk in 1298 was terrible. Culloden in 1746 was grim and wiped out the whole Highland way of life, but Flodden wiped out a whole generation of Scots. There must have been few families who did not lose a son, a father, a brother or a husband.

After Bruce, James IV was the most beloved monarch that Scotland ever had. He was handsome, enigmatic, a poet and a warrior, and a great patron of the arts.

In 1513 the English invaded France, and in lieu of the Auld

Alliance between Scotland and France, an alliance originally designed to counteract English aggression to its neighbours, north and south, the Queen of France beseeched James to intervene. She sent James a note asking him to advance into England and break a lance for her sake, and sent him a gold and turquoise ring. James had a very chivalric side to his nature and raised his army to answer her call. They gathered on Edinburgh's Burghmuir. Marching south, they crossed the Tweed at Coldstream, using the fords here that so many armies of invasion into Scotland have used over the centuries. The gold and turquoise ring of the Queen of France was to cost a fortune in the lives of the menfolk of Scotland.

James's army only advanced a few miles into England, and, apart from assailing a few local castles, did little else, except to wait for the Earl of Surrey to advance with an English army north, to bring the Scots to battle. James's army outnumbered the English and they had by far the best of it when it came to ground. They held the higher land of Flodden Hill. The English crossed the River Till and were on the lower ground between the Scots and the border. The Scots moved *en masse* to Branxton Hill. Had they attacked the English as they crossed the Till they would have utterly destroyed them, but the moment was gone.

There was an exchange of cannon fire, and for some mad inexplicable reason the Scots marched down the steep slope of Branxton, towards the English positions, giving up all their superiority of higher ground.

It had been raining, and the Scots kicked off their shoes to try and get a grip on the wet grassy hillside. The Scots found that their long spears were a terrible hindrance on the slope, unbalancing them. At the bottom of the hill they came up against the ranks of their enemy, and they were armed with the bill, a long axe with a curving hook at the back. They were able to use the hook to pull down and lop the speartips from the Scots' weapons. The Scots were soon surrounded, and the English worked steadily. The huge ring of Scots round James IV was growing steadily smaller.

As a teenager I knew a little about James IV and had read Tranter's *Chain of Destiny* which describes James's life. Around this time I started to read the works of HV Morton. Morton wrote a travelogue of a tour of Scotland in the 1920s and it is a rattling good yarn of the glory days of driving, before today's congested roads. He spoke of Flodden, but one line in particular jumped out at me. He asked, 'How many Scots know that the sword, ring and dagger taken from the body of James IV are in the College of Arms in London?' I had no idea what the College of Arms was, so I looked it up. It is the English equivalent of our Lord Lyon Court – in other words, the place where coats of arms are registered and conferred. The building was constructed to replace an earlier one that was destroyed in the Great Fire of London. Looking up everything I could find on the place, I discovered that when the new building was opened in 1671 in what is today Queen Victoria Street, the direct descendant of Surrey, the victor of Flodden, gifted the sword, ring and dagger found on the body of James IV to the College. Surely, although it was 158 years after the battle, this Surrey would know exactly what he was donating and where it came from. It should also be noted that these direct descendants are patrons of the College of Arms and so have a vested interest in the place.

I eventually managed to gain access to the College of Arms. As I had no real reason for being there it did take a little subterfuge to get to see the items I really wanted to see. They asked me to sign the book. I couldn't resist writing 'James Stewart' in the space. They had no real idea what I was talking about at first but eventually they came to the conclusion that there was a sword in one of the rooms that might be the one I was after. They took me through to show me. There was a case that I can only describe as a big rectangular fish tank. It had various objects inside – a couple of Zulu clubs, if I remember rightly, and a sword. It was a hand-and-a-half sword, with long curling quillions. And a dagger. Clearly it and the sword were a matching pair: same shape, only scaled down, same curling quillions (the sort of cross-bit to protect the hand, for those who aren't familiar). Beside these two objects was a ring. It was a gold and turquoise ring. The Queen of France sent James IV a gold and turquoise ring. Did James wear it during the invasion and have it on at Flodden? I looked at it. It was a bit bashed. Was this the very ring that caused a whole generation of Scots to die on Flodden field? It occurred to me that I was perhaps the only Scot to have seen these items since 1513. I was enthralled. But surely rather than being locked away in a building in London where nobody was particularly interested these items should be on show in Scotland, where people certainly would be interested. After all, the Common Riding ceremonies that take place in our Border towns are connected to Flodden and its aftermath.

By chance I was asked to do the oration on Flodden battlefield in 1995. I had not realised that it was such a large event. I had never really spoken in front of an audience like this before, in the open and on a battlefield, and for the weeks leading up to the event I was petrified. It went well, though, and I spoke about the sword, ring and dagger as part of my presentation. It caused a flurry of interest. When I finished, my driver for the day asked, 'Where to?' (I don't have my own driver – the good people of Coldstream had hired me a nice big black Merc complete with driver for the day!) I replied, 'The first pub in Scotland – and step on it!' He obviously had not been asked to step on it very often, and so did, much to the delight of a motorcycling speed freak like myself. So I reached the Besom, the first pub over the border, and got ready to calm my nerves. Just then a couple of old boys slid a whisky in front of me. One of them said, 'I've listened to speeches on that hillside man and boy, but you made me proud to be Scottish today, so let me buy you a drink'.

Thank you. The weeks of worrying and then having to stand up in front of that crowd, never really having done anything like that before, were suddenly made OK. He was a Scot and was proud of *me*. I couldn't have asked for a better start and Flodden became the first of many such speeches. His thanks were worth more than gold to me and his thanks alone were enough. As various people who had been on the battlefield drifted back to Coldstream, enquiries were made to me regarding James's artefacts. This interest developed over the next few months and eventually an enquiry was made from museums in the Borders to the College of Arms asking if it would be possible to have a loan of the items. Eventually they said yes, but a large sum of money would be needed as surety. This money was eventually put in place. Then the message came back that the items were not authentic, or that the sword might be but the dagger was not. How could this be? They were a matching pair.

The Scots side of things then had to pull out of the deal as they could not put up money for items that were not authentic. Why ask for a large sum as surety if the items were not the real thing? All very strange.

I'm not blind to the ins and outs of all this. The English are obviously going to view the sword, ring and dagger as spoils of war, and after all they were captured on English soil. But if we are all 'British', then surely the items should be allowed to come north?

Later communications from the College of Arms say that the sword and dagger are of a later era than Flodden, and this has been verified by the Armourers at the Tower of London. Again, why demand surety? I find it hard to believe that the patron of the College would gift artefacts, captured by his ancestor, that he knew to be false, or that he had made a mistake about their authenticity. I looked at that gold and turquoise ring, bashed and misshapen, and knew. It was just too much of a coincidence.

The sword, ring and dagger are still kept at the College of Arms.

On Flodden battlefield, the ring of English bills scythed into the Scots foot soldiers. They died in their thousands around James. Surrey and his commanders sat atop a small rise. James had been wounded several times, pierced by arrows, and one hand was now hanging by a strip of flesh. He knew that the only hope now was to try and slay Surrey. If their commander was slain the English might lose heart. He slashed and cut his way forward using his one good hand. He was drawing nearer to Surrey. Surrounded by a group of Scots fighting like men possessed, he fought to within just a metre or two of his foe. 'One spearlength', as the English chroniclers stated. James readied himself for the final lunge but an archer standing by Surrey's shoulder let fly, and as James opened his mouth in a final shout of defiance, ready to cut Surrey down, the arrow actually went in and pierced his neck. So fell one of Scotland's finest kings, and his countrymen died around where he lay until darkness made more killing impossible.

The next morning James's body was pulled out from the pile of dead, and those who knew him recognised the body and swore it was the King of Scots. He was first carried into the little church at the bottom of the hill at Branxton. This little church survives to this day, some of it the original building from the day of the battle. From here he was conveyed to Berwick. For the rest of the thousands of Scots dead, huge pits were dug, and the bodies were unceremoniously piled in. Some are next to the church, others are buried nearer the later monument to the fight. I was recently shown aerial photographs of the area and the burial pits can clearly be seen as darker rectangles on the landscape. James's body was disemboweled and embalmed, sent to Newcastle where it was placed in a casket of lead, then conveyed south to London. Catherine of Aragon sent on the bloodstained surcoat to Henry VIII, who was at this time in Flanders. James's body was sent to the Monastery of Sheen in Surrey, where the leaden coffin was kept in a side room with old timber. Stow, who was a writer of these times, penned a book on London that is still available. It is an easily read guide to these days and most people with an interest in history will find it fascinating. Stow describes how he actually saw the body of the King of Scots at Sheen, and how workmen cut off the head, purely for fun. The site of Sheen Monastery is now the Royal Mid-Surrey Golf Club, standing on the River Thames.

Lancelot Young, Elizabeth I of England's master glazier, was intrigued by the head of James IV. It was still red-haired and bearded and gave off a pleasing scent. He took it to his London home as a conversation piece. We don't know what became of the rest of the body of the King of Scots – we can only assume it was buried at Sheen. After a time, Lancelot Young was persuaded to give up the head, or grew tired of having it, and as St Michael's Church in Wood Street in the City of London was clearing bones out from the charnel house of the crypt and burying them in a large grave in the churchyard, James IV's head finally came to lie with a pile of English bones. St Michael's stood until the early 1900s. Certainly it was in a state of ruin in 1902. The site of the church, until the late 1990s, had a building containing offices of British Telecom, but at time of writing this building has just been demolished. It came as a bit of a surprise to find that the land here is owned by Standard Life of Edinburgh. Strange that the Flodden campaign began with the army amassing on the Burghmuir of Edinburgh and ended with James's head being buried on land now owned by an Edinburgh company. A new building is planned for the site, which now bears the address 2–12 Gresham Street. I am pleased to inform that an archaeological exploration of the site is under way. The odds of anything that we can connect with James being found are, of course, astronomical, but the knowledge of what this site contains has been brought to the attention of Standard Life and they are considering marking the site in some way, perhaps with a plaque. The *Scotsman* newspaper also picked up on this story and covered it in their edition dated Tuesday 11 January 2000, devoting over half a page to it, with a follow-up the next day.

The twists and turns of history never cease to amaze me. The College of Arms is not too great a distance from the site of St Michael's in Wood Street. It is strange that James's head should eventually lie not so very far from where his artefacts ended up, and of course both ended up in London, travelling from Flodden's battlefield. Both are also only a short walk away from the memorial at Smithfield where Sir William Wallace was cruelly murdered. This might be something visitors to London may wish to bear in mind.

Surrey, the victor at Flodden, had gifts bestowed on him for his annihilation of the threat from Scotland. He was 'promoted' to Duke of Norfolk and his coat of arms was changed. It now contains the 'top half' of a lion rampant, a sawn-off Lion Rampant of Scotland no less. And this lion is transfixed by an arrow going in through its mouth and out through the back of its neck. Perhaps it is just me, but I find this quite insulting. I cannot recall ever having seen any Scots family who has managed battle victories and honours over England or the English adding anything that could be construed as demeaning towards their foes in any way. Surely chivalry would demand otherwise?

Flodden field today holds that certain indefinable something that battlefields which remain relatively untouched seem to retain. Taking the road south and crossing the River Tweed at

Coldstream on the A697, the battlefield is signposted from the main road. The little village of Branxton nestles at the hillfoot of the ridge that the Scots commanded. The little church where James's body was taken stands nearby, with its great pits where so many Scots whose stories we do not know lie for eternity. Slightly past the church stands the monument, overlooking the whole scene, looking up to the ridge down which the Scots advanced down, and looking down into the dip where the worst of the carnage took place. If you return to the village and take the junction where there is a little farm road striking south, which runs up towards the ridge of Branxton where the Scots stood, you cross a tiny burn in the dip before the gradient upwards starts to steepen. It was here, to your right, that the casualties were the greatest. If you look west along the course of the tiny burn, the rise on its northern side was where Surrey stood, and it was, of course, on the side of this rise that James, King of Scots, the fourth of that name, died transfixed by an arrow through the mouth. He is remembered, though. There is a group that commemorates the battle on the field every year. But I think the real loss of Scotland's menfolk comes across to me when I read books of Scots' castles and their histories. Nearly every one has, in its story, the Third Earl, or the Fourth Baron, or the Second Laird who was slain at Flodden – a whole generation gone. And the wind continues to sigh across the grassy slopes of Branxton Hill, and across the graves of so many Scots who died within sight of their homeland but lie in foreign soil.

Religion

SCOTLAND MUST BE the only country in the world where if you ask a child what the opposite of blue is they would answer 'green'! I was taken to Ibrox to see Rangers often when I was a kid, and I must have only been twelve or so when I realised that a Union Jack flies over one end of Glasgow and an Irish tricolour flies over the other. What's all that about?

I'm a Scot. Knew it from a tender age, so couldn't identify with these people putting another nation before their own. I find it embarrassing to watch either of the two big Scottish teams playing in Europe on TV, seeing those flags *en masse*, instead of the flag of Scotland. I've heard all the excuses before: 'I'm British, therefore I'm proud to fly the Union flag'; 'Celtic were formed from Irish stock, so I'm proud to fly the tricolour'.

What do foreigners make of it all? I have tried to explain the bigotry to foreign visitors, but there is no point – I can see the blank looks on their faces. They cannot comprehend such a thing. It has never occurred to me to find out the religious persuasion of the people round about me. There are good and bad in every group of people, and if people are decent to me, that's fine.

But in Scotland there is the strangest of twists to the way religion is perceived.

When Celtic were playing Inter-Milan in the European Cup Final of 1967, Rangers supporters watching the game on television in bars in Glasgow were heard to exclaim 'Get into these fenian bastards' when Inter scored. The fact that Celtic were fielding Protestant players and Inter were, obviously, a Catholic team, did not seem to register, or if it does it seems Scots Catholics are somehow different from foreign Catholics.

I swear this next bit is true. I was once giving a talk about Wallace and at the end when questions were being directed to me about the great man, I was asked, 'That Wallace was a Tim [Scots slang for a Catholic], was he not?' I gently explained that all Christians over Europe were Catholics at that time. 'He was still a Tim', came the reply.

And yet holding extreme religious views does not equate with attending church or chapel in Scotland. The majority of the most vociferous advocates of their particular camp don't actually worship. It's as if the Scots need something to fight about. After all, the Scots have always been happier fighting each other than taking on anybody else. Perhaps it's like the old inter-clan warfare. It has gone, so this is a replacement.

I am glad to say, though, that most Protestants and Catholics seem to be mostly content with shouting abuse at each other for the duration of the game then working alongside each other the next day with no major trauma. You get the occasional fanatic right enough, but, as I say, there are good and bad in every group of people. Enough of the present; let's look back at the coming of Christianity to Scotland.

There were what are known as pagan religions in Scotland before the Christian religion appeared. Many churches in Scotland are actually on old pagan sites. There is a church near my home that sits in a circular churchyard. This is probably the site of an ancient stone circle and the church was deliberately built on this site to stamp out the 'old ways', and to take advantage of a site already regarded as 'special'. I notice these all over the country. Another obvious one is at Lamington on the upper Clyde, and it is possible that the Marion Braidfute of legend, Wallace's sweetheart, is buried there.

The first church built in Scotland that we know of was the White House of St Ninian or, as it is sometimes called, Candida Casa. As is usual in Scotland, there is debate about where this building stood. As the Scots like arguing, it is as if there is divine providence involved. Some say it was in Whithorn, where the ruins of the priory church stand. Others say it was at the Isle of Whithorn nearby, where the ruins of a later chapel still stand, on the coast.

No matter where the original Candida Casa stood, the priory at Whithorn saw the visits of many Scots royals on journeys of pilgrimage. Bruce was here shortly before he died. James IV visited every year, and sometimes twice yearly, until his untimely death at Flodden.

St Ninian founded this church as early as 397AD, and he died and was buried in his church in 432AD.

St Columba, the Dove, is the most famous of our missionaries. He came to Scotland and set up a small monastery on Iona in 563. Columba was actually an Irish princeling, and came to Iona to try and atone for the blood he had shed during acts of war in Ireland. Iona was the first place he landed where he could not see the mainland of Ireland on a clear day. This was part of his atonement. Columba's influence on his adopted home was to be huge. Iona became the burial place of the Kings of Scots. Columba came to Scotland from Ireland; oddly enough, Ireland's patron saint, St Patrick, was born in Scotland, at Kilpatrick on the Clyde, the name a corruption of the Cell of Patrick, referring to the monks of that time residing in little beehive 'cells'.

Columba preached a religion of compassion, a faith that preached forgiveness. Strange that one thousand years on, Scotland replaced this with the face of stern hard Calvinism. 'Thou shalt not . . !' became the cry.

The one big problem I have with the Reformation is the destruction that was caused. So much destroyed in the name of advancement – and so little tolerance in that advancement! Buildings destroyed. Ornamentation smashed. Even tombs, including that of Bruce, shattered by hammer-wielding mobs. What the hell were they thinking of? Idolatry that needed to be cleansed? Surely using one's artistic ability is a celebration of life. I can't stop thinking about how rich a cultural inheritance and understanding of times past we would have in Scotland if the destruction that went with the Reformation had never taken place.

But destruction follows destruction, and John Knox, the man who incited so many of those mobs to destroy, is now said to be under the car park behind St Giles Cathedral in Edinburgh, his tomb gone like so many others. On my last visit he had a Volvo parked on top of him. It's a funny old world. And where have we gone since the Reformation? Schisms, and even sterner forms of worship.

One of my favourite wee stories is the one about the minister who takes over a parish in the Western Isles. After his Sunday sermon he decides to take a stroll and enjoy the air. As he passes a croft, one of his elderly parishioners comes out to remonstrate with him. 'Minister!' he cries, 'what are you doing out strolling on the Sabbath?' The minister replies, 'Didn't our good Lord himself enjoy a walk after church on the Sabbath?' 'Yes, and the people of this parish have never thought the better of him for it', came the reply.

So, where do I stand in all this?

Well, I believe in the one commandment. 'Do whatever the hell you like as long as you don't mess up anyone else's life in the process'.

In other words, if you want to ride a motorcycle at 150 m.p.h., don't do it where you are going to kill someone.

If you want a wild time, have it, just make sure no one else gets messed up in the process.

If you want to worship your own particular brand of religion, do so – but don't ram it down anyone else's throat.

Makes sense to me.

At least we don't have *too* many fanatics in Scotland. We can't really be bothered with jihad and fatwah. Rather go to the pub to be honest – and talk a good fight on occasion!

Poor Mary Queen of Scots, though. Head chopped off in the name of religion. She was accused of treason, yet if she was indeed as much of a threat as has been made out the English would not have beheaded her. The threat of retaliation from Catholic countries like Spain or France would surely have been a worry.

Glasgow has quite a few memorials to Mary that most of the citizens seem all too unaware of. Just across from the ruins of Cathcart Castle stands a stone marked m.r. (Mary Regina) which marks the spot where Mary stood to watch the ill-fated Battle of Langside.

Glasgow council, in their wisdom, demolished this castle in the 1970s for no apparent reason. It was a ruin but was complete to the wallhead, and I'm sure many interested parties would have loved to have mounted a restoration.

Not long prior to this they demolished Castlemilk, which stood only a couple of kilometres away. It was inhabited right up to demolition, and its low remains stand in a children's park in the Glasgow scheme of that name.

The monument to the Battle of Langside stands behind the Victoria Infirmary, and the fight took place on the hill leading up to the memorial. When Queen's Park was being laid out, it was decided to build the boating pond on an existing marsh. Common sense. As digging in this marshy area adjacent to Pollokshaws Road commenced, the workmen uncovered bodies, skeletons of horses, even scraps of armour. It turns out that this was the burial pit used for the dead after the battle. Obviously, when the fight was over and orders went out to bury the dead, some bright spark remembered the nearby marsh and decided to use that. Common sense. The ground around the memorial, which stands on a hilltop, would have been tough to dig into, so the marsh made sense. Often when I am searching for sites it is the use of a procedure as simple as this which finds them. What would I have done if I were there on the day? Look around for possibilities.

You might want to remember all those poor souls next time you are out in an 'oary-boat' on Queens Park pond.

Cathkin Braes on Glasgow's south side also has a Mary stone. The view over the city is spectacular here. It is claimed you can see half the population of Scotland. Mary supposedly rested upon this stone to admire the view.

The level of religious unrest over the years in Scotland, from the Reformation till Culloden, is quite astonishing. There were the campaigns of James Graham, the Marquis of Montrose. His is one of the first signatures on the Covenant, copies of which are in various parts of the country. There is one in St Giles Cathedral, by Montrose's tomb. No visitor should miss it; a remarkable likeness, beautifully carved from white marble, and said to be the most exquisite tomb of this period in Scotland. Montrose believed in the Reformed religion, but he did not believe in the beheading of Charles I, and did everything in his power to uphold his loyalty to the Stewart line. Like Wallace, his name is scattered over the face of Scotland, only in his case it is from the Borders to the far north. Montrose fought a myriad of battles before his shameful betrayal at Ardvreck Castle by Loch Assynt, from where he was taken to his execution in Edinburgh. Like Wallace, his body was cut to pieces, but after the restoration of Charles II as much of his body that could be found was gathered for his tomb in St Giles.

It is strange that Montrose is buried on the southern side of the church while his great enemy, Archibald Campbell of Argyll, is buried on the northern side. I find it bemusing to walk from one side to the other, just a matter of metres separating these two as they lie for eternity. It is like having Wallace and Longshanks buried in one building, the difference being that Wallace was a freedom fighter while Montrose was a religious freedom fighter. The one detail regarding Montrose that shines is the loyalty of the man. Like Wallace, Montrose would not be swayed from his chosen course, no matter the odds. If only we had more in our history like him. Greyfriars Kirk (as in Greyfriars Bobby!) is only a short walk from St Giles, and they have in their possession there a sword that was carried at Montrose's execution, as well as their own copy of the Covenant.

Covenanters' graves and monuments are scattered over Scotland. The south-west is positively littered with them. So many who were prepared to die for their religious beliefs, yet just a few hundred years on church attendance is falling and all over our cities empty churches are falling into ruin.

Why has religion died away so drastically in Scotland? For over a millennium it was the prime mover in our history. David I was a great abbey-builder. Wallace was a religious man. Bruce had his heart taken on crusade. Nearly all the Stewarts engaged in pilgrimages. Mary died for her religious beliefs, and ordinary men and women suffered great religious persecution again and again over the centuries. But it would seem our psyche has changed in the last century or so. Capitalism and commercialism are the new religions, it would seem. People live for *now* and do not question the hereafter, just as history and a sense of being does not seem to matter much either. The old ties of kinship and clan, and the geneaology of you and yours, and where you came from, can seemingly also be ignored in modern consumerism.

But we need to know history to learn.

I see traditional styles of housing being shunned for houses designed for the south of England. Housing estates of English-style brick housing are springing up all over Scotland. No one roughcasts any more. But the roughcasting keeps out the damp and frost. Scotland is damp – that's a fact we are all too well aware of. The damp permeates brick, then when the frosts come and the damp freezes, the brick crumbles. Roughcasting prevents this, but it is hardly used in the building of new houses today. This is part of the *unlearning* process in Scotland, where the past is ignored.

One year I heard the leader of the body of horsemen at Flodden shout to the riders as they got ready to ride off, 'Remember lads, you are Scots – and you didnae come fae nothing!' I wish more would take that on board.

So what has me rambling on about architecture got to do with religion? Very little, unless I include the design of many of our modern churches in there somewhere. Another piece of the unlearning process. Look at Glasgow Cathedral – the present building was founded in the twelfth century and has survived the worst the Scottish weather has thrown at it over the centuries. I'd be surprised if many of the modern glass and wood structures will last for fifty. St Bride's Church in East Kilbride is one of these modern places of worship. Constructed only forty-odd years ago out of red brick, the architect was acclaimed and the structure itself won awards for its innovative design. It had been up less than thirty years when the steeple was demolished as it was unsafe. The rest of the building needs constant maintenance. Please, building planners; some of your ideas are a case of 'nice building, wrong country'. I see these modern churches crumbling away. But perhaps they are not built to last? For better or worse, religion is a fading entity in Scotland, but these buildings seem to be fading even quicker than their congregations!

Union and On and On

KING JAMES VI OF Scotland inherited the throne of England in 1603. You would think that this would have brought Scotland into the ascendancy, but history proves that the greater always consumes the lesser, and with England having ten times the population of Scotland, and probably many more times that when it came to monetary wealth, absorption was inevitable. King James is often referred to as the 'Wisest Fool in Christendom'. His shambling gait and slovenly ways hid a quick, learned and inquisitive mind. His English Lords referred to him privately as 'The Scotch Monkey'. He was responsible for the translation into modern language of the Bible, which explains why, when you open most copies, it has 'King James Version' stamped on the flyleaf. Much to my surprise, on opening a Mormon Bible it also has 'King James Version' written within. Apart from being the man who gave us the modern Bible, James gave us such other diversions as witch-burning on a grand scale, and he upset Catholics in England so much that the Gunpowder Plot was devised to blow him to kingdom come. On reflection, though, I've just realised that a Scot is also responsible for 'Bonfire Night' – see, I told you we invented nearly everything!

Although governed by one monarch, Scotland and England were still separate entities, though the word 'Britain' was starting to creep into everyday usage. James himself seemed to be happy to call himself 'King of Britain'. Britannia was the Roman name for England, while Scotland was Caledonia, but for some reason 'Britain' became corrupted to encompass the whole island.

Royalty continued down to James's son and heir, Charles I, but Charles was dethroned and executed, and 'Britain' was suddenly under the grip of Oliver Cromwell.

Cromwell was 'no friend of Scotland', to put it mildly. At the Battle of Worcester in England many Scots were slain. But the biggest shock came at the Battle of Dunbar on 3 September 1650, and I'm afraid we are back to the old story. We learnt absolutely nothing from history.

In 1296, the opening battle of the Wars of Independence was fought at Dunbar. After the infamous Sack of Berwick, the English advanced up the east coast of Scotland and besieged the castle at Dunbar. The Scots army advanced and held the heights of Doon Hill, just inland from Dunbar itself. For some stupid reason the Scots yielded their unassailable position and came down from the hill to be cut to pieces on the well disciplined and well ranked English army below. Three hundred and fifty-four years later, Cromwell occupied Dunbar and its castle. The Scots again held the height of Doon Hill behind the town. The Scots army numbered twenty-three thousand to Cromwell's eleven thousand, but again they gave up their strong position and marched down to be annihilated by the disciplined English.

Four thousand were slain and ten thousand were taken prisoner. Incredible. Not only had the same mistake been made twice, but had been made twice in the same location! Why didn't they learn from prior mistakes?

Even worse was to follow. The prisoners were taken south in a week-long nightmare. Fifteen hundred either died, escaped or were killed. On 11 September (a very important day in Scotland's history – but more of that later), three thousand were counted into the cathedral at Durham. The Scots had supposedly fasted for up to eight days before Dunbar, and some had eaten raw vegetables while passing Morpeth and it made them ill. There were no facilities or warmth provided for these captives, and it was not long before dysentery spread. Hazelrig was an ominous name to Scots – this one was the descendent of the man whom legend states murdered Wallace's sweetheart Marion. Certainly Wallace revenged himself by slaying him at Lanark. This Hazelrig reported on 31 October that out of the three thousand prisoners at Durham, only six hundred remained, the rest buried in a mass grave in a ditch that had been dug as a latrine. This grave was rediscovered in 1946 when central heating pipes were being put into a nearby music school. Of the survivors, many were used as slave labour in English iron works, or were banished to the vicinity of Boston in the USA.

A monument to the 1650 battle was raised in 1950, a roughly carved stone which bears some words of Carlyle: 'Here took place the brunt of essential agony of the Battle of Dunbar'. It stands in the area of Dunbar called Broxburn, a little north of the A1.

Cromwell was determined to subjugate Scotland. To try and effect this, he built five great fortresses, at Leith, Perth, Ayr, Inverlochy and Inverness. These edifices cost the best part of £100,000 each to construct – a vast sum in those days. The fort at Inverlochy formed the basis of the later Fort William, the name eventually being transferred to the nearby town. There is a remnant of the Ayr fortifications visible just in front of the Citadel Leisure Centre on the south side of the mouth of the River Ayr.

But Cromwell's biggest disservice to Scotland, other than killing many of its citizens, was his acquisition of all the records and documentation he could lay his hands on. In his role as 'Lord Protector' he had this lot taken to London whence it would never return. Many of these documents were placed aboard a ship which then sank. This was a huge loss. It left so many gaps in our nation's recorded history that accounts of various circumstances and times were lost forever.

If the past is partially destroyed, it causes a weakening of what we are. This is why the loss of our archives is devastating.

Edward Longshanks had pulled exactly the same stunt, stripping Scotland of its records at his time, and taking them south where they disappeared. As already said, a country is the result of its history.

Cromwell and Longshanks were brothers in that respect.

But I'm a great believer in the old adage 'what goes around, comes around'. Longshanks is a man reviled in Scotland today. He did all in his power to destroy Wallace, scattering his body so that he could not rise on Judgement Day – a widely held belief in those days.

Scotland loves Wallace. I attend Wallace marches and ceremonies all over Scotland. I can see the passion for the man and the solemnity in the faces of those involved. Who cares about Longshanks today? I don't see 'Longshanks ceremonies' taking place.

Cromwell got his own strange comeuppance. He died on 3 September 1658, the anniversary of both his battles where he killed many Scots – Worcester and Dunbar. He was embalmed and buried in Westminster Abbey. A plaque in the Henry VII chapel says it is 'The burial place of Oliver Cromwell 1658–1661'. But the tomb has gone, because after Charles II's restoration it was decided to dishonour Cromwell as much as possible. His body was exhumed and dragged in its shroud through London from Holborn to Tyburn, long a place of execution. The gallows at Tyburn I see mentioned again and again in English history. I often wondered where Tyburn stood as I noticed it was not on modern maps of London. It turns out Marble Arch is right on the site. Many of the victims, once dead, were buried here to dishonour them. Strange that this is now the most affluent part of London, being in the vicinity of Park Lane.

Cromwell's rotted corpse was hung here for a time, then beheaded. The body was buried near the gallows, the exact spot being the junction of Connaught Place and Connaught Square. Cromwell's head was displayed on a spike at Westminster Hall, above the building where Wallace's sham trial took place.

During James VII's reign, the head was blown down in a storm and taken home by a guard, who then sold it on as a curiosity. It changed hands a few times for ever-increasing sums of money, and was eventually given to Cromwell's old college at Cambridge.

Incredibly, it was 1960 before Cromwell's embalmed head – still in a recognisable state with the hair of the skimpy beard and moustache, as well as the famous wart still visible – found its last resting-place. It was buried in the chapel of Sydney Sussex College, Cambridge. The exact spot of the burial is a secret but a plaque at the chapel door reads: 'Near to this place was buried on 25 March 1960 the head of Oliver Cromwell, Lord Protector of the Commonwealth of England, Scotland and Ireland, Fellow Commoner of this College 1616–17'.

Later in the 1600s there were many upheavals in Scotland. Many fights threatened the Union of the Crowns in 1603, notably Killiecrankie, where there is now a visitor centre recounting the story of that battle, where the claymore and Lochaber axes of the Highlanders are said to have killed two thousand redcoats in two minutes flat! Much of this upheaval was directed against William of Orange, another who was no friend of Scotland, yet some Protestants in Scotland today refer to him as 'King Billy', as if he

The bell tower at the ruins of Cambuskenneth Abbey. The Abbey was the supply depot for the Battle of Bannockburn. Bruce's body lay here the night before its arrival at Dunfermline. Legend states that Wallace's left arm is interred here, and the tomb of James III and his queen stands at the high altar.

The tomb of James II and his queen, Margaret of Denmark. It stands at the high altar in the ruins of Cambuskenneth Abbey.

The coffins of 'James VIII', Charles Edward (Bonnie Prince Charlie) and his younger brother Henry, which lie in a vault below their memorial in the Vatican. The wreath was laid by a member of the Tartan Army (Scotland's football supporters) and it is a cuff of a Highland jacket belonging to one of them that can be seen on the right-hand side of the picture. (Photograph courtesy Tartan Army)

Falkland Palace in Fife. James V died here.
His body was taken to Holyrood Abbey in Edinburgh for burial.

Monument to Thomas Muir of Huntershill, the famous radical.
It stands opposite the family house.

A gathering on Bonnymuir to commemorate the skirmish that ended the 1820 uprising. The slogan on the banner, 'Scotland Free or a Desert', was one used at the time.

The Stone of Destiny crosses into Scotland in 1996, seven hundred years exactly since it was looted and taken south over the River Tweed here by Longshanks.

The pillar in memory of James Wilson, one of the 'ringleaders' of the 1820 rising, stands on the site of his house in Strathaven, near the entrance to the town cemetery.

were a saviour. William actually took the crown through tenuous links with the House of Stewart, the Royal House of Scotland, long before the Union of the Crowns. He showed his demeanour towards Scotland during the 'Darien Scheme', or, as it is sometimes known, the 'Darien Disaster'. The ins and outs of it upset me when I first heard of it as a teenager, and the more I have discovered since then, the more it has upset me. Darien was a brilliant idea and it is no wonder that so much of the nation's money was sunk into the project. After all, the Scots' ideas for the land known as Darien eventually came to fruition in the shape of the Panama Canal. Honestly! We could have been contenders.

We have produced so many brilliant engineers since that time that building a canal across the Isthmus of Panama must have been feasible even for early settlers. One wee fact that has always intrigued me, strange though it seems, is that the Pacific end of the canal is actually further east than the Atlantic end. This is due to the twists and turns of the isthmus itself.

What is not commonly known is that many Scots settled in the Gulf of Mexico before Darien. There was a large colony on Barbados, for instance. In fact, Paterson, the mind behind the scheme, had spent some time in the Bahamas. He was well-travelled for a Dumfriesshire boy.

I have been to Florida at the height of summer and have stood on the shore of the Gulf of Mexico and gazed over towards Panama, sensed, but far over the horizon. The humidity was overwhelming and I was at least able to sense how it must have been for those Scots settlers having to work at everything to survive.

In museums it is possible to recognise coinage issued by the 'Company trading to Africa and the Indies', as the company set up to colonise Darien was known, because there is a wee setting sun (perhaps its a rising sun?) at the base of the coins.

The ships that set out for Darien left from the port of Leith. We can imagine the populace gathered on the quayside to watch them depart on their great adventure. Three of the ships were fitted out as men-of-war. They had patriotic names: the *Caledonia*, the *St Andrew* and the *Unicorn*. These were joined by two tenders laden with provisions.

William of Orange, or, as he now was, William II of Scotland

and III of England, was to demonstrate his lack of love for Scotland. He saw Darien as a challenge to the business of the Dutch East India Company and the trading power of England and went out of his way to lay obstacles in the Scots settlers' path. He made it clear that any attacks on Darien would elicit no aid from England. When the Spanish mounted an attack on the Scots' settlement, one of the Scots, Captain Campbell, assailed them with two hundred Highlanders. Though sixteen hundred strong, the Spanish were routed with much slaughter. When news of the failure of Darien reached Edinburgh, there was uproar. But the Edinburgh mob was excited at the news of the settlers' slaughter – under Campbell – of the Spaniards. The popular cry went up that all the houses in the city should be lit up in recognition of this deed, so proud were the people of this display of 'the auld Scots Spirit'. The mob then marched through the city looking for windows that were unlit, and when one was discovered it was smashed. They managed to cause £5,000 worth of damage at 1700 prices! Politicians were threatened, and demands were heard that the Scots crown should be withdrawn from William. In return, the authorities demanded the Edinburgh hangman should be flogged for not punishing the rioters. The executioner of Haddington was hired to inflict the punishment but refused to flog his brother hangman from the capital. The magistrates of Haddington, scared of losing face, then had their own hangman flogged. This innocent man, therefore, took all the punishment for an Edinburgh riot that could have led to a civil war and the ousting of William II.

There are still place names in Panama that are a throwback to the Darien Scheme – Punta Escoces, Caledonia Bay and the Caledonia Mountains. There are still the remains of the Scots settlement, the growth of jungle flora now covering them. An archaeological expedition was mounted in 1979 and it located all the main buildings. I'll just have to take others' word for that, though, as I haven't managed to get my motorcycle that far yet!

Scotland, money-wise, was brought to its knees after the collapse of Darien. The country was bankrupt.

It seems strange that the freedom that every other nation has battled for since the dawn of time should, in Scotland's case, have been decided by the stroke of a pen. Well, not only a pen, but a substantial amount of money changing hands in a surreptitious manner. 'We are bought and sold for English gold', wrote Burns.

The bankruptcy caused by the Darien Scheme was very much a deciding factor in this, and yet much of that disaster was caused by English intervention – or lack of – when it was really needed. The people of Scotland were firmly against the Union, of course, resulting in riots in the streets of Edinburgh and Glasgow. But the people had no say in the outcome. Some of the great and good tried to do their best for their ancient northern realm, particularly Andrew Fletcher of Saltoun, a name proudly remembered for his loyalty. Fletcher argued long and hard for the retention of Scotland's independence in the days leading up to the Union. He did all in his power – making eloquent speeches, petitioning other members of the Scottish parliament to make the right decisions for Scotland's good – but he saw the bribes offered from England taking their toll, and the Union was forced through. I can imagine the utter devastation that Fletcher must have felt, seeing his beloved nation sold down the line. Fletcher had other talents too. He caused great advancements in agricultural improvements, seeing possibilities to increase Scotland's monetary wealth through better farming practices. His home was originally an old fortified building, modernised and extended in the early nineteenth century. It is still a private house. The two nearby villages are West Saltoun and East Saltoun. Fletcher was buried in the family vault in the church at East Saltoun. The site is ancient; the original building was a dependency of Dryburgh Abbey but the building today is a Gothic-style edifice with a tower and ninety-foot spire dating from 1805.

I am glad to say that every year a commemoration of Fletcher's work for Scotland is held in the village.

See – people do care!

Scotland's last parliament rose on 25 March 1707, never to meet again until the Yes-Yes vote of 1997 had its effect. It saw impassioned pleas by the Duke of Hamilton and Lord Belhaven in defence of liberty. Lord Belhaven made a speech in which he stated that the Scots were now slaves forever and that the Union was an entire surrender. He actually dropped to his knees in tears, begging fellow peers not to betray their country. He was answered by the pro-Union Earl of Marchmont, who said sneeringly, 'Behold, I dreamed, and lo, when I awoke, I found it was a dream.'

This sums up so much of the turmoil inherent in Scotland that seems to have been there through the ages. What is it that makes some Scots love and believe and others to put another country's ideals above their own? I have never understood it. Absolute betrayal is anathema to me. How must Wallace have felt? How must Belhaven have felt at the condescending reply to his pleas?

The articles of the Union were pushed through.

The Cameronians, a regiment raised by Protestants in south-west Scotland, marched into the town of Dumfries and at the market cross they burned a copy of the Articles of Union, along with the list of commissioners who signed it. They intended to march on Edinburgh but were betrayed by spies – and the insurrection petered out.

Many of the Articles of Union have since been broken, or disregarded. One of these was Article 16, which stated that there should always be a separate mint in Scotland. Although the coinage was now the same in both countries, Scots' coins struck at the mint in Edinburgh were distinguished by the addition of an 'E' beneath the portrait of Queen Anne, who was now on the throne. For some reason it was not felt necessary to put identification marks on coins struck in London. Crowns, half crowns, shillings and sixpences were struck in 1707 and 1708. By 1709 only half crowns and shillings were struck. These were the last coins produced in Scotland. The mint then remained dormant and was abolished in 1817, the building finally demolished in 1877.

The first coins were struck in Scotland in the reign of David 1 in 1136, and for six hundred years each monarch produced their own. For those interested, the Hunterian Museum, within Glasgow University, has a large collection on show, and many smaller museums have collections of some sort. I love to look over these remnants from the many different ages of our history. I especially like the early 'hammered' coins, made simply by striking bullion with a hammer and die.

I recall bumping into a numismatist (coin collector to you and me) one day and asking which coins are particularly sought after. 'Coins from the Holy Land from about 2,000 years ago', he replied.

'Why?', I asked naïvely.

'Because Jesus might have held them', was the obvious reply.

This is the attraction for me. I try and imagine the hands that once held these Scots coins. Wallace? Bruce? Mary Queen of Scots? All from a time when Scotland was a real separate entity.

Jacobite Years

THE EARL OF MAR, who led the Jacobite forces at the Battle of Sheriffmuir, was born at Alloa Tower, which stands in the town of the same name. The site it commands is not especially defensive but it is an imposing structure and it has walls ten feet thick. It was constructed during the reign of David II, between 1360 and 1380. It has recently had much restoration work done and it is open to the public from April to September. The tower is signposted from the town centre.

The Earl of Mar was referred to by the nickname 'Bobbing John', due to his ability to duck and dive and to change sides as the climate suited.

The Battle of Sheriffmuir itself was fought on a western shoulder of the Ochils, a little above Dunblane. The battle has gone down in our history books as a draw, both sides managing to overcome one wing of the other, with the result that neither side was too sure who was the victor.

The easiest way to visit the battle site is by taking the unclassified road, signposted Sheriffmuir, from the large roundabout in Dunblane that was on the route of the old A9 (the town has been bypassed by a modern stretch). This small road runs right through the battle site and again meets the A9 further north at Blackford.

By this road, as you cross the battlefield, you come across a large memorial cairn. It is the Clan MacRae stone, dedicated to the men of that clan who marched from the far north-west of Scotland to take part in the fight. It bears an inscription in English and Gaelic, the Gaelic for the clan being MacRath, or 'Son of Grace', the name probably having an ecclesiastical origin.

If you take the path that runs down behind this monument, then veer south-west, you come to the 'Gathering Stone of the Clans' standing in the middle of a clump of old trees. The Highlanders who took part in the battle are said to have met here to whet their dirks and claymores on this large whinstone block before the fight – not an unreasonable assumption. The stone is enclosed by an iron grating, with a brass plate attached, gifted by a Mr Stirling of Kippendavie in 1840.

In 2000 I did the oration at the Clan MacRae stone at the annual commemoration of the battle. It was an evening of total blackness and some of the heaviest driving rain I have ever seen. The attendees at this event were all in plaids and weaponry, and every second person had a burning pitch torch held aloft to light the scene, out on the rainswept moorland. I looked out over this scene and imagined some tourists suddenly coming across us all. I knew how we looked, rain dripping from beards and all those sodden tartans and burning torches. Walking into this you would have been hard pressed to recognise reality. You would have thought you were seeing a window from history. Only in Scotland. Again, sometimes it is brilliant to be Scottish, even if your leather is soaked with the rain and you couldn't have got wetter jumping in a river. Such events are what memories are made of.

The Sheriffmuir Inn stands on the battlefield, and, although they are a memento of earlier times, it is worth mentioning the 'Wallace Stones'. They stand in the dip north-east of the inn, and although nearby are not visible from the road. These are a row of standing stones, obviously quite ancient, and traditionally they mark where Wallace's men gathered before advancing to the Abbey Craig and the Battle of Stirling Bridge. This is feasible. We know that Wallace and Murray were besieging Dundee when word of the advance of the English came. So many men would not have been ferried over the Tay; they would have headed to Perth, then out south through Dunning and up onto Sheriffmuir. A landmark is needed for a rendezvous and these stones were as good as any. There is running water nearby and plenty of ground for camping, but it has a remoteness that would have kept the army hidden from prying eyes. I love the way all the eras interconnect. It just brings home the fact that Scotland is just as it was, and the roads and glens that our ancestors walked are the same we recognise today.

After I had written my Wallace and Bruce books, my publisher asked if I could 'do' Bonnie Prince Charlie as a follow up. For better or worse, he is one of Scotland's big names, so I decided to give it a bash. My knowledge of sites associated with Charlie was greater than I first realised. Just travelling the roads of Scotland had given me a grounding, but there were many places in England that I was hazy on or not too familiar with.

It was just a case of getting out there and travelling the known routes. It's a strange thing to be able to do, I suppose, but I can close my eyes and see every step of the way from Glenfinnan to Derby to Culloden. I just wanted to bring the landscape to life for people, so they would know that momentous events had taken place in that field at the side of the motorway, and so on. I was not interested in the ins and outs of the politics, or, for that matter, the religion. Religion is about people's heads and thoughts – I wanted to concentrate on the martial and physical aspects. I stated at the beginning of the book that I had shied away from these topics as much as possible. But, as probably expected in the recesses of my mind, I did get letters of complaint because it was felt I had glorified a Roman Catholic. These letters contained condemnation of every aspect of Charles's personality. What do people want? Are we meant to sanitise history so that only the bits that suit people are left?

The more I looked into Charles, the more I could see of the propaganda machine at work. After all, the Jacobites were the losers, so the victors, the Hanoverians, were obviously going to demean them as much as possible, with Charles's degeneration into alcoholism in later years a useful stick with which to beat him.

Charles stood six feet tall and the distances he covered in the course of a day over hard mountain country I found quite extraordinary. In a prior life I spent much of my time 'Munro-bagging' and have a reasonably intimate knowledge of much of the Highlands, and I understood just how great were some of his undertakings. In exile in France he introduced boxing to the general public, something I never mentioned in the book, but wish I had. As Charles himself often stepped into the ring, this, coupled with the fact that he was a brilliant shot with both the gun and the bow, should, I hope, dispel the 'effeminate Franco-Italian' image that seems to pervade many Scots' minds.

The 'heavy' religion tag attached to Charles does not seem to exist either. He seemed happy to tolerate religious freedom, not seeming deeply religious himself. He did convert to Protestantism after the '45, and remained a Protestant until almost his life's end. He probably converted to further his dynastic claims but it does show that his religious convictions were not great.

A lot of people take umbrage with Charles because of the misery his failed campaign caused. Although by the standards of many Scottish battles the death toll at Culloden was not vast, it was the opening of the floodgates for the destruction of the clan system and the Highland way of life. All those empty straths and glens. All those sheep.

One cannot but wonder what the situation today would be if Charles had not been determined to pursue his claim to the throne. Would the depopulation of the Highlands have been inevitable anyway? Of course, it was all a gamble. If Charles had succeeded the Highlands would have benefited. But people in Scotland blame Charles because it was his personal ambition that caused this downfall.

Robert the Bruce took part in a very similar gamble but succeeded, therefore he is seen as a saviour and hero to people today.

No matter. The Highland Clearances began, and the children of Scotland are scattered over the New World.

I felt really very sorry for individuals I met in Canada, descendants of the Clearances, who had visited Scotland and who really thought that their surnames would still matter today – and not just in the Highlands. One woman I met was a descendant of the Border clan of Elliot. She had recently visited Scotland, 'the Auld Country', and had gone into pubs in the Borders announcing she was an Elliot. She was met with blank stares where she thought she would be welcomed with open arms. She was confused by this, and spoke to me about it. How do you explain that most folk in Scotland don't give a toss about their surname or their heritage? She had been brought up in Canada being told it was important. And the saddest thing of all is that I think they have it right.

Later Years

AFTER THE FAILURE of the various Jacobite uprisings, the Government in London began to harness the fighting power of the Gael and various Highland regiments were formed. It is strange that over the intervening couple of centuries proud traditions have sprung up and these regiments are now identified with Scotland. Strange, because many of them were raised either to suppress other Scots or to fight in foreign lands against peoples with whom they themselves had no argument. The fighting abilities of Scots have never been in doubt, but many times in Scotland's past the leadership was. London took this on board and these regiments helped colour red great chunks of maps of the world, denoting the British Empire. Most people are probably familiar with the expression 'The sun never sets on the British Empire', coined because the Empire itself was so far flung that at any time the sun was shining on part of it.

For obvious reasons I have always been more interested in the history of Scotland before the Union. I was once doing a talk about the Wars of Independence, talking about Scotland as a nation state and so on. An English gent in the audience was trying to impress upon me the importance of England where Scotland was concerned. In the middle of this he reiterated, 'The sun never sets on the British Empire'. I retorted, 'That's because God doesny trust the English in the dark.'

Sometimes I have my moments. The audience liked it at any rate.

The French Revolution had an impact on Scotland that today is largely forgotten. The assertion that all men are equal and had a right to say how they are governed took a grip on the imagination of the country. The works of Robert Burns, of course, echo this sentiment – 'A man's a man for a' that'. Paris itself has always held an attraction for me. It has so many threads intertwined with Scots history and the Auld Alliance. James, the Black Douglas, who carried Bruce's heart on crusade and who is a great hero of mine, was raised in Paris to keep him from Longshanks' clutches. When I look at Notre Dame, for instance, I imagine him seeing it too. Wallace was here, Mary Queen of Scots was here, and various Scots' artefacts have been brought here over the years. The first time I went to Paris, the bus from the airport dropped me at my little hotel near the Sacré-Cœur. I walked in to register and as soon he heard my voice the attendant on the desk said, 'Robert the Bruce and the spider!' in a strong French accent (of course, because he was French). I never realised that it was such a widely known story and it was the first thing that jumped into his mind when he realised I was Scottish.

By chance, I discovered the catacombs under the city, a network of tunnels dating back to Roman times. During the Great Terror in France that followed the French Revolution, so many died that there was no room in the graveyards to bury them all, so they put the bodies down in the old catacombs. The entrance is in Montparnasse. You descend down an old stairway into the tunnels. Eventually I reached a door, a sign above proclaiming 'La Ville de la Mort'. As I entered this city of the dead, I walked into a nightmare world that I could not have pictured in the darkest recesses of my mind. There are eight million bodies down there. Even in skeletal form the sheer number is staggering. We know what a football crowd of fifty thousand looks like – well, eight million skeletons take up some amount of space. Many of the bones were piled in bizarre sculptures, dozens of grinning skulls in artistic shapes. It took a long time to walk through it all. Certainly took away my appetite for a long time. It was almost impossible to realise that each of these rickles of bones was once a person with hopes, fears and dreams like us.

Many of the ordinary people of France obviously paid a high price for their *liberté*. Thank God that the same did not take place in Scotland. We've had some right baddies in our time, but luckily we never had Robespierre.

The idea of freedom contained in the French Revolution certainly did strike a chord with many Scots, and the spread of the written word that took place at this time also helped. Many tracts and pamphlets were published that helped to raise awareness among the lower classes of Scotland, and many of those spoke out against the current policies of the London Government.

It is also worth remembering that the oldest newspaper still being published, anywhere on the planet, is the Aberdeen *Press and Journal*. Second is Glasgow's *Herald*, and the third is the London *Times*.

The best known and most meteoric of the Scottish radicals of this time is Thomas Muir (1765–1799). Thomas was born the son of a Glasgow merchant. The family built themselves a house named Huntershill in the Bishopbriggs area of Glasgow in 1770 and Thomas was raised there. The house still stands, in Crowhill Road, near Bishopbriggs railway station. The original house has been extended and is used as a pavilion for the nearby playing fields, but the original part of the building in the centre looks very much as it did in Muir's day. Thomas studied and practised law in Glasgow and Edinburgh, eventually becoming a noted reformer connected with the Friends of the People and the United Irishmen. His influence in Scotland coincided with revolutionary events in France. He was taken into custody on 4 August 1793 and was tried in Edinburgh on 30 to 31 August for libel and making seditious speeches. Much to the surprise of many people he was given the harsh sentence of 14 years' transportation to Australia's Botany Bay. He landed there after a delay in London, in October 1794. The short remainder of Muir's life reads like a story in a novel. He managed to purchase a thirty-acre farm but only stayed on it for fourteen months. In January 1796 he managed to convince the captain of an American ship to take him across the Pacific Ocean to Boston. Once he hit the coast of America he got himself transferred to a Spanish ship which was bound for California, which at that time was under Spanish control. He hoped that the Spanish authorities would grant him a United States passport, but they refused, and treated this Scots radical with such suspicion that they arranged for him to be taken to Spain. But as the convoy carrying Muir approached Cadiz in April 1797, it was attacked by British ships, as 'Britain' and Spain were now at war. Muir was badly wounded and was taken to a military hospital. The French authorities heard that Muir was in Spain and asked the Spanish for his release to their care, and this happened in November 1797. The French treated him as a hero and he began to embroil himself in Scottish affairs once more. He beseeched the French Government to send an army to liberate

Scotland. The French certainly took an interest in Muir's proposals but all debate was cut short at his early and untimely death in Chantilly in January 1799. He was only 33. Opposite Muir's house at Huntershill stands a memorial which was unveiled in 1996. It bears a bust of Muir and the following lines:

> I have devoted myself to the cause of the people. It is a good cause. It shall ultimately prevail. It shall finally triumph.

A tall obelisk to Muir's memory stands in the old Calton Cemetery in Edinburgh but it is not often mentioned in guidebooks to the city. It seems Muir is regarded as *persona non grata* in some quarters, due to his revolutionary beliefs.

In August 1819, the populace of Paisley heard of political unrest taking place in England. Sixteen thousand of them protested on Paisley's Meikleriggs Moor. The Provost told them they would not be allowed to march through the town displaying their banners, and a riot broke out. The band that was present got locked up for playing *Scots Wha Hae*. This was a marching song that dated back to the time of Wallace and Bruce, the words written at a later date by Robert Burns. It was played before Bannockburn, and now Scots were jailed for playing it! The result was that Scots everywhere began to whistle, hum and sing it in defiance.

But the uprising that most Scots seem to remember happened the following year, in 1820. In April of that year word spread that a rising was to take place and that troops based in Glasgow were to be the initial target. The talk was that between five and seven thousand radicals were going to gather on Cathkin Braes overlooking Glasgow on the south, and that a similar group would be assembling in the Campsie Hills to Glasgow's north. Suitably encouraged, about a dozen men set off from Strathaven to head towards Cathkin Braes. They carried a banner they had made which stated 'Scotland Free or a Desert'. Almost two millennia before, Calcagus had stated 'You Romans come here, create a desert and call it peace!' – directed against the mighty Roman Empire. This time the handful of men comprised simple weavers and the protest was directed against their own government, not based in Scotland but in London.

At East Kilbride the group learned that the uprising had not occurred. It is believed that all the talk of insurrection had actually been spread by the government to force radical Scots out in the open. In hope more than anything else, they continued on to Cathkin, but found no one there.

In Anderston in Glasgow, a small group *had* gathered. It was decided to head along the route of the Forth and Clyde Canal to try and seize the Carron ironworks, one of the main manufacturers of ammunition in Scotland. These works, on the River Carron, manufactured so many cannon for use aboard ships that a salvo of fire at sea is known as a 'carronade', rather than 'cannonade', the term used on land.

The Glasgow group, led by Andrew Hardie, linked up with another small group at Condorrat near Cumbernauld. This new group was led by John Baird. They walked on in the rain and passing Castlecary were spotted by a trooper who galloped to the garrison at Kilsyth, warning them what was happening.

Just past the village of Bonnybridge, on Bonnymuir, the hussars from Kilsyth caught the radicals. They wounded four and took the other forty-seven prisoner. Between them, the prisoners had five muskets, two pistols and eighteen pikes.

The government in London did not think that the Scots would deal with these acts of 'treason' to a satisfactory degree, so they sent up a special commission to apply English law in Scotland. Another Act of Union broken. This court moved from Stirling to Glasgow, from Strathaven to Paisley, and from Dumbarton to Ayr to dispense justice. Under the English Law for High Treason it found eighty-eight people guilty. Most were handed sentences of transportation. Three were given the death sentence. Andrew Hardie and John Baird were executed in Stirling. A monument to their memory stands in Sighthill Cemetery in Glasgow. James Wilson, who had been a member of the march from Strathaven to Cathkin Braes, was the third. He had done little on this occasion but was a long-time reformer and so his execution was a simple way to get rid of a nuisance. He was hanged in Glasgow, then the executioner cut down his body and hacked off the head, holding it aloft and crying, 'The head of a traitor'. There were cries of 'murder' from the crowd. Beneath the steep hill leading up to the cemetery in Strathaven stands a monument marking the site of the house of James Wilson. Every year the 1820 Society remembers, through various commemorations, the men whose watchword was 'Scotland Free or a Desert'.

Insurrection was not yet dead in Scotland. Just after the end of the First World War, profiteering, appalling housing conditions and landlords pushing up rents had the ordinary Scot ready to revolt. The Russian revolution was a fresh event, and Scotland had its own revolutionary leader in the shape of John MacLean. Militants in manual industries in Glasgow began to be called 'Red Clydesiders', and MacLean, who had undergone periods of imprisonment for his beliefs, was recognised as their leader. MacLean announced that he would make Glasgow 'a Petrograd, a revolutionary storm centre second to none'. It came close to happening, or at least the threat of it happening was enough to make the authorities in London react, and react harshly. A mass demonstration was held in Glasgow's George Square on Friday 31 January 1919. The government response was to site a Howitzer field gun before the doors of the City Chambers and tanks were housed in the building that today houses the city's Tramway Theatre. It was like an early Tianamen Square. Most shocking, though, were the machine-gun nests mounted on top of George Square's Post Office building, now converted to flats, and the Copthorne Hotel, next to Queen Street station. Violence broke out in the square below and it was dealt with by repeated baton charges from the police. I once spoke to a man whose father knew one of the soldiers sited in a machine-gun nest above the square. His father had asked the soldier what he would have done if the English officers had commanded the Scots gunners to open fire on their many thousands of fellow Scots below. He said that he had already spoken to his fellows regarding this eventuality and they had agreed that if the order to fire had come, they would have killed their officers. Luckily the order to fire never came and Scotland was spared the bloodbath that had engulfed so much of Europe over the preceding years.

Freedom of a sort did reach Scotland of course, with the Yes-Yes vote for a Scottish Parliament to reconvene – the first time since 1707 – taking place on the 700th anniversary of Wallace's victory at Stirling Bridge, 11 September 1997.

The results of this vote were announced the following morning, and that day I was, by pure chance, giving a talk at a Braveheart convention taking place in, of all places, Stirling. John and Linda Anderson of Edinburgh had organised this event and many of the stars of the film were in attendance. I had to give a speech about the life of Wallace with slides and so on, and I finished by hammering out *Scots Wha Hae* on the guitar. I came close to losing it emotionally several times. I had dreamed of seeing Scotland gain some sort of autonomy since I was a kid, and it had come to pass. I thought of Wallace, and what he would think; 700th anniversary of his great victory, too. But much more important than any of this was that Scotland had gained at least a little constitutional change, and it had been done through the ballot box and not violence. So few nations seem to have gained change by democratic and peaceful means that it made me proud of my people.

The day the new parliament actually opened was also spent in the Stirling area, as I was helping with a programme at the National Wallace Monument, speaking to the world about changes taking place in Scotland.

I would have liked to have been in Edinburgh, watching the festivities, but there was something very special about standing at the monument, looking up at the mighty statue of Wallace, his sword held aloft.

Did I see a wry smile flash across his face?

The Way Forward

DONALD DEWAR DID it. He delivered when many over the years had promised and all came to nought. Donald is rightly called the 'father' of the Scottish Parliament. He will be remembered in our history books. I met him once, at the reburial of the heart of King Robert the Bruce at Melrose Abbey. Donald was well read and knew his history. I believe he was a real patriot and was passionate about his nation and its past.

I have oft wondered if Donald was perhaps the man responsible for choosing 11 September as the day of the Yes-Yes vote.

I was a kenspeckle figure in my kilt, and he came over for a chat once the ceremony was over. It was an important day. A leaden casket containing what is believed to be Bruce's heart had been excavated at Melrose. It was taken to Edinburgh for various tests and then, rightly, it was returned to Melrose in a new casket to be buried with honours. It lies underneath a round plaque in the abbey grounds bearing the legend 'A noble heart may have no ease if freedom fail', words taken from Barbour's *The Bruce*, written in 1370. Well, I might not have shared Donald's politics, but he sure as dammit had a noble heart. Imagine being able to say that you managed to gain some sort of autonomy for your country. Donald did just that. He died far too soon, far too early.

I have seen politicians speak in the US (they may seem cheesy to our jaundiced Scottish sensibilities, but they are damned good at it) and they know how to pull an audience in and hold them in the palm of their hands. Most of our politicians look shoddy in comparison, like social club conveners.

I've heard people knock Tommy Sheridan. I don't completely share Tommy's politics either. But I believe that he believes. And that matters.

The people who go into our history books are not the good people who do their best every day of their lives. The nurses, or firemen who take terrible risks. The pen-pushers who keep the wheels of finance turning. The people who go down in our history books are the ones who go against the grain. The rocks who were prepared to stand in the middle of the stream. The ones who said 'no' when all those around were saying 'yes'.

Tommy Sheridan is a rock in the middle of the stream. And Tommy is the type to go down in our history books. He is prepared to take a stand for what he believes is right.

We do have some who are in the political arena for all the right reasons, however. But political personalities aside, where does Scotland go from here?

How do we take Scotland forward to statehood again when that statehood is blocked deliberately by the very politicians who should be serving our country?

There are many in Scotland who do not regard themselves as Scots. They think of themselves as 'British'. This should be borne in mind.

Back in 1997 I got into a discussion with an American woman whilst on one of my many visits to the National Wallace Monument. She asked me why my country was subservient to another. I scrabbled for answers. But then she told me a story. She said that she had been watching TV here and it was immediately apparent to her that Scotland was talked down, and talked down to, constantly. I think a lot of what is said on TV washes over us and we don't realise just how bad it can be at times, though she could see the bias clearly. She spoke to me of the times of the American struggle for independence from the control of the British. She explained that one third of the American population was firmly on the side of patriotism, and wanted independence for their emerging country. It does seem ridiculous that a country three thousand miles away was in control of a land as vast as the US. Another third of the population was firmly on the side of being ruled from Britain, and I suppose saw themselves as being 'British'. The remaining third did not have a particular bias one way or the other. She continued, telling me that those who wanted independence managed to convince enough of the third who did not have a particular affiliation to come out in their favour, that the change came about, and the USA came into being.

Perhaps the situation in Scotland is not too different. We seem to have a third of our population who are patriotic Scots, people who believe in their fellows and their homeland, and who love it enough to want to see it free. We seem to have another third who regard themselves as Britons and not Scots, people who feel that Scotland is better served by being part of a bigger conglomerate, and that the union is best for Scotland's population. I don't care for this attitude. But that should not come as a shock to anybody! The decisions taken for the greater mass are not necessarily best for Scotland's well-being. If I'm honest, that has nothing to do with it, really. I'm a Scot, born in Scotland. And I wish freedom for my people.

The other third in Scotland don't really seem to care one way or another. In fact – and I think that if people here are honest I won't get too slated for this – a large number of Scots don't care much about their nation's situation as long as they have the price of a pint or a packet of fags in their pocket.

There are clearly the downtrodden in society too, who have enough trouble existing day to day to have energy left to worry about the national or political climate, and that is understandable.

But to get back to the American lady, it would seem that the way forward for Scotland is that the third who do care deeply need to persuade enough of the third who don't care one way or the other that their way is the right way. Education is the key. I have always found that those who have even a basic grounding in Scotland's history tend to feel passionately for her well-being. I have never met anyone who has learned her story and thought less of her future!

But I must add that I have no fear of the third who regard themselves as 'British'. I know that a wider understanding of Scotland will see their numbers dwindle, not multiply. Every person I have ever met, and I have met many, who has been well versed in their country's story has her basic freedoms in the forefront of their psyche. It seems that education is the way. At school I learned very little of Scotland's story. I educated myself by travelling around our hilly little country and avidly reading all I could get my hands on that told her story. Imagine if our kids were given that basic grounding at school and grew up knowing that the blood that runs in their veins has seen so very many adventures in the past, a past that they share with their class-mates. In the USA or Canada, or Turkey for that matter, the national flags are everywhere. American kids are imbued with a pride in their basic freedoms and nationhood.

Our kids should have the same access to pride. Every Scottish school should fly the Saltire, and every single child should be able to tell me what being Scottish means, what their flag means, and should be able to take any other child from any other nation in the world and grip them by the hand as a brother or sister – because they are equals, and because they have the same inherent pride in where they come from.

Odds and Sods

I HAVE BEEN LUCKY. Sometimes I have been able to do things that were really a dream come true for me. I was always *really into* the Wars of Independence, and when my Wallace book was published, Elspeth King, curator at the Stirling Smith Art Gallery and Museum, allowed me to launch it there. It's nice to do something like that in a town so steeped in Scotland's story, and also it is so close to where he won his great victory at Stirling Bridge. I released the Wallace book in February 1999. I was thirty-nine. I would like to have done something similar at a younger age, but it took me that long to gain all the information needed and to visit, never mind discover, all the places contained within the book.

The Bruce book was released in June 1999. It was launched at the Bannockburn Heritage Centre on the actual anniversary of the battle – the 685th to be precise. This was a real big deal for me. I never thought that such an opportunity would come to me, and felt that somehow I had forged just a tiny connection with Bruce and the Scots who fought with him on that day.

I want people to realise that our history is not just a collection of tales. It is real lives and real people. We are the result. Part of me was there. If you are a Scot, part of you was there too. At the Bannockburn launch I was lucky to have Hugh Robertson with Fire and Sword, his battle re-enactment group. The auspciousness of the location was not lost on them and Hugh had a 'rerr terr' running about in his Lion Rampant surcoat – Robert the Bruce for a day.

My Charlie book was launched in Autumn 2000 and I was lucky enough to do a double – a Glenfinnan event on one day and then Culloden the next. Glenfinnan, of course, is where the standard was raised, signifying the opening of the Jacobite campaign of the '45, and Culloden was the battle where all the Stuart hopes were to be dashed forever.

The staff at all these locations were helpful and enthusiastic, and all very knowledgeable about their history, so I'm glad they

humoured me and didn't try to shoot me down in flames!
I have had some strange coincidences take place on my
journeying. I once climbed Ben Nevis in midwinter. Glen Nevis
was full of snow, and the depth was immense when the summit
was gained. I climbed inside the shelter by the summit cairn to
find that there was already an occupant. I remember he mentioned he was from Largs, and he gave me a toffee. I next climbed
Ben Nevis the following autumn in glorious sunshine. When I
reached the summit there was an individual already there. As I
approached him he began to stare. 'Do you come up here every
day?' he asked. I realised that it was the same guy from Largs
from several months before. He had not been up 'the Ben' since
the last time we had met – and neither had I. It seems incredible
that of all the people in the world, and many thousands from
many different nations climb the Ben every year, I should meet the
same person twice in a row in the same place, he arriving a
minute or two before me. And what's more, he recognised me. It
was only when he mentioned giving me a toffee that I realised
who he was.

When I was younger and poorer, and in between motorcycles,
I still had a yearning to explore Scotland and I used to hitch-hike
around the countryside, even sleeping rough on occasion. I once
hitched a lift just at the bridge over the Dee, on the main route
leading south out of Aberdeen. As I stuck out my thumb a lorry
stopped almost immediately. I did not hitch-hike again for quite a
few months. The next occasion was at Hamilton. I stuck out my
thumb and a car stopped almost immediately. As I climbed in I
could not believe that the car driver was the same guy who had
picked me up in the lorry the last time I hitched, at the other end
of the country.

Graffiti is another source of constant amusement to me. I've
seen some memorable daubings on my travels, but these must be
the two most bizarre. In Skye promoting the Charlie book, I saw
scrawled on a wall 'Big it up for the Portree Massive!' Shades of
the black ghettos of the USA in the Hebrides? Taking the bike
across to Islay on the ferry, I went for a pee (you know the sort of
thing, white painted toilets, all bulkheads and portholes). I
noticed this message written with a big black felt pen on the toilet

wall: 'Mull are Wanks!' What, the whole island?
Scottish artefacts abroad. Flicking through books I have discovered that many important fragments of our history are in far-
flung locations. The Great Seal of Robert the Bruce, which shows
him sword in hand astride his charger, bedecked in Lion Rampant
surcoat, became the basis for the equestrian statue at
Bannockburn. This seal is kept in the Bibliothèque Nationale in
Paris. James IV had a beautiful ornate triptych, a portable altar,
bedecked in jewels with the most exquisite paints. This triptych is
in a museum in Vienna. Surely these would be better appreciated
at home? If freedom for Scotland comes we should look at ways
to return what is ours and they should be on display for the
descendants of the people who created them. As we have seen,
many of the burial places of royalty are also abroad. Perhaps St
Margaret's remains should be returned to Dunfermline Abbey
along with those of her husband. This all works both ways, of
course. I have always believed that the Elgin Marbles, looted from
the Parthenon in Athens, should be returned to their original location. Sure, we need artefacts of other cultures in our museums so
that people can learn, but there are limits.

I have a wee concern for the constant erosion of things
Scottish, some of which I have seen decay over the last thirty
years, since I was a kid. If something was good, we said it was
'brammin' or 'teakin'. Kids today, indoctrinated by the barrage of
US-made television, simply say 'cool' to everything. The language
my peer group used has disappeared in a decade or two.

I have seen the erosion of our place names. It always seems to
be referred to as the Clyde Valley – it's Clydesdale! I have even
noticed a sign stating 'Welcome to the Liddesdale Valley' – it is
Liddesdale! The name is self-explanatory – it does not need
'valley' tacked on the end for the benefit of tourists. I like the
difference!

It's a shame, really. The world is not only growing smaller, but
it is slowly being taken over by a single culture. If you go into a
room in a Holiday Inn in Glasgow, Hong Kong, Rome or New
York, it is the same lamp that sits on the same table. People are
becoming like that too. It's the same jacket, same trousers and
same shoes no matter the country. And if you ask them what they

think of something, if they like it they'll probably reply 'cool'.

When I was seventeen and one of my friends came back from a holiday in, say, Italy, and told me he had made the aquaintance of an Italian girl, I would have asked immediately, 'What was she wearing?', 'What music did she listen to?'. But there is no point any more. She will be wearing the same clothes and listening to the same music as any Scots teenager.

Vive la différence – that's what I say.

It's not that I want Scots to think they are better than anyone else. We aren't. But we are Scots. We're not better than the Dutch, Tibetans, Argentinians or New Zealanders – but we're *different*. And long may it continue. I happily wear my plaid on occasions – weapons too, if the situation warrants it – and everyone knows right away what nationality I am.

In April 2001 I visited Chicago where I was doing talks on Scotland's history as part of the Tartan Day celebrations they have in the US. I flew over to Washington too, to see Sean Connery being awarded the 'William Wallace' award on the steps of the Capitol Building. It is given to the Scot who has done most to forward Scottish–American relationships each year.

Back in Chicago, I got a call to tell me my next event was on the ninety-somethingth floor of a building on Michigan Avenue. As the hotel I was staying in was just off Michigan Avenue, I enquired how far along Michigan the gig was, to see if I should get a taxi. 'Only a block or so', I was told. I decided I would walk rather than call a taxi.

You see, *sgian dubhs* are not permitted to be worn in the States, and I was carrying enough weapons to stage my own minor war, but if it was only a block or so to walk I figured I'd get away with it.

I had had a confrontation in Brussels airport on the way to Chicago when I was asked if I was carrying anything sharp. As I opened the cases containing my swords they were completely nonplussed and unsure about what to do with me – but I digress.

I donned my plaid, strapped on various swords and dirks, and slipping my arm through the straps of my targe (embossed Highland shield) I stepped out into the Chicago streets. As I reached Michigan Avenue, I realised, looking at the numbers, that my destination was at least a mile down the street.

Bugger! I thought, but I started walking. It was about five in the evening and all the offices were emptying. Crowds of people pointed and gawped. Cars screeched to a halt. I just tried to look ahead and keep going. Folks stared, or whooped as I passed by.

As I approached a junction, I spotted two cops, heavily armed, raising their sunglasses to stare. I feared the worst. I envisioned being run in, or perhaps they would shoot me and ask questions later. They beckoned me over. As they did, one whispered in the other's ear. 'You a real Scotchman, boy?', one enquired. 'I am', I replied. 'Prove it!', he stated, making a motion with his hand that I should raise my plaid. I put down my targe and lifted the folds of tartan to prove I was wearing nothing but a draft, in front of several hundred interested onlookers. He turned again to his compatriot, laughing, and said, 'Told you!', and the pair walked off laughing.

I'm tired of people slagging off the tartan, haggis and heather image of Scotland. It's immediately, recognisably Scottish. Every other nation on earth would *kill* to have the identity we have. It is nothing to be ashamed of. We have a culture that can be worn, looked at, even eaten or drunk! What have the poor English got? Morris dancing? Beefeaters?

When I was younger it almost seemed somehow second-class to be Scottish.

Not any more.

The day will come when we have pride again, when the Saltire will fly alongside the flags of other nations on an equal basis.

There is only one thing I ask of you all. It had better happen in my lifetime!

Postscript

11 SEPTEMBER. A special day in the history of Scotland. The day of Stirling Bridge. The day 700 years later when Scotland took its first tentative steps towards its destiny. 11 September is to all intents and purposes Scotland's Independence Day. That all changed when the Twin Towers and the Pentagon were hit by terrorists.

11 September, for the foreseeable future, will be associated with those attacks and I feel it is unfortunate that for years to come, as commemorations take place at Stirling Bridge and the vote for our parliament is remembered, we will also be thinking of the darker memories of that day. Those responsible for these atrocities inadvertantly erased a little of what it means to be Scottish.

This saddens me. Please take pride, and please remember your history.

It matters.

Some other books published by **Luath Press**

On the Trail of William Wallace
David R. Ross
ISBN 0 946487 47 2 PBK £7.99

How close to reality was Braveheart?

Where was Wallace actually born?

What was the relationship between Wallace and Bruce?

Are there surviving eyewitness accounts of Wallace?

How does Wallace influence the psyche of today's Scots?

On the Trail of William Wallace offers a refreshing insight into the life and heritage of the great Scots hero whose proud story is at the very heart of what it means to be Scottish. Not concentrating simply on the hard historical facts of Wallace's life, the book also takes into account the real significance of Wallace and his effect on the ordinary Scot through the ages, manifested in the many sites where his memory is marked.

In trying to piece together the jigsaw of the reality of Wallace's life, David Ross weaves a subtle flow of new information with his own observations. His engaging, thoughtful and at times amusing narrative reads with the ease of a historical novel, complete with all the intrigue, treachery and romance required to hold the attention of the casual reader and still entice the more knowledgeable historian.

74 places to visit in Scotland and the North of England
One general map and 3 location maps
Stirling and Falkirk battle plans
Wallace's route through London
Chapter on Wallace connections in North America and elsewhere
Reproductions of rarely seen illustrations

On the Trail of William Wallace will be enjoyed by anyone with an interest in Scotland, from the passing tourist to the most fervent nationalist. It is an encyclopaedia-cum-guidebook, literally stuffed with fascinating titbits not usually on offer in the conventional history book.

David Ross is organiser of and historical adviser to the Society of William Wallace.

Historians seem to think all there is to be known about Wallace has already been uncovered. Mr Ross has proved that Wallace studies are in fact in their infancy.

ELSPETH KING, Director of the Stirling Smith Art Museum & Gallery, who annotated and introduced Luath's edition of *Blind Harry's Wallace*.

Better the pen than the sword! RANDALL WALLACE, author of *Braveheart*, when asked by David Ross how it felt to be partly responsible for the freedom of a nation following the Devolution referendum.

On the Trail of Robert the Bruce
David R. Ross
ISBN 0 946487 52 9 PBK £7.99

On the Trail of Robert the Bruce charts the story of Scotland's hero-king from his boyhood, through his days of indecision as Scotland suffered under the English yoke, to his assumption of the crown exactly six months after the death of William Wallace. Here is the astonishing blow-by-blow account of how, against fearful odds, Bruce led the Scots to win their greatest ever victory. Bannockburn was not the end of the story. The war against English oppression lasted another fourteen years. Bruce lived just long enough to see his dreams of an independent Scotland come to fruition in 1328 with the signing of the Treaty of Edinburgh. The trail takes us to Bruce sites in Scotland, many of the little known and forgotten battle sites in northern England, and as far afield as the Bruce monuments in Andalusia and Jerusalem.

67 places to visit in Scotland and elsewhere
One general map, 3 location maps and a map of Bruce-connected sites in Ireland
Bannockburn battle plan
Drawings and reproductions of rarely seen illustrations

On the Trail of Robert the Bruce is not all blood and gore. It brings out the love and laughter, pain and passion of one of the great eras of Scottish history. Read it and you will understand why David Ross has never knowingly killed a spider in his life. Once again, he proves himself a master of the popular brand of hands-on history that made *On the Trail of William Wallace* so popular.

David R. Ross is a proud patriot and unashamed romantic SCOTLAND ON SUNDAY

Robert the Bruce knew Scotland, knew every

class of her people, as no man who ruled her before or since has done. It was he who asked of her a miracle – and she accomplished it.
AGNES MUIR MACKENZIE

On the Trail of Bonnie Prince Charlie

David R. Ross

ISBN 0 946487 68 5 PBK £7.99

On the Trail of Bonnie Prince Charlie is the story of the Young Pretender. Born in Italy, grandson of James VII, at a time when the German house of Hanover was on the throne, his father was regarded by many as the rightful king. Bonnie Prince Charlie's campaign to retake the throne in his father's name changed the fate of Scotland. The Jacobite movement was responsible for the '45 Uprising, one of the most decisive times in Scottish history. The suffering following the battle of Culloden in 1746 still evokes emotion. Charles' own journey immediately after Culloden is well known: hiding in the heather, escaping to Skye with Flora MacDonald. Little known of is his return to London in 1750 incognito, where he converted to Protestantism (he reconverted to Catholicism before he died and is buried in the Vatican). He was often unwelcome in Europe after the failure of the uprising and came to hate any mention of Scotland and his lost chance.

> 79 places to visit in Scotland and England
> One general map and 4 location maps
> Prestonpans, Clifton, Falkirk and Culloden battle plans
> Simplified family tree
> Rarely seen illustrations

Yet again popular historian David R. Ross brings his own style to one of Scotland's most famous figures. Bonnie Prince Charlie is part of the folklore of Scotland. He brings forth feelings of antagonism from some and romanticism from others, but all agree on his legal right to the throne. Knowing the story behind the place can bring the landscape to life. Take this book with you on your travels and follow the route taken by Charles' forces on their doomed march.

Ross writes with an immediacy, a dynamism, that makes his subjects come alive on the page DUNDEE COURIER

Blind Harry's Wallace

William Hamilton of Gilbertfield

ISBN 0 946487 43 X HBK £5.00

ISBN 0 946487 33 2 PBK £8.99

The epic verse of Blind Harry (or Henry the Minstrel) is the earliest surviving source on the life of Wallace, yet it has been out of print for most of this century. It was written around 1477 and based on the now lost Latin writings of Thomas Gray and John Blair, commissioned by 'the fechting bishop' William Sinclair, Bishop of Dunkeld, to send to the Pope. Blind Harry sang or recited his stories of Wallace all over Scotland and attracted the support of James IV, who ordered his work to be printed. *Blin Hary's The Actes and Deidis of the Illustre and Vallyeant Campioun Schir William Wallace* was one of the first Scottish books printed in Scotland.

Hamilton's edition, 'wherein the old obsolete words are rendered more intelligible', first published in 1722, was almost certainly the most widely read book in eighteenth-century Scotland after the Bible. It had a great influence on Burns (whom it inspired to visit many of the sites mentioned and to write a number of poems including *Scots Wha Hae*) and many others.

Elspeth King has long campaigned to bring Blind Harry's work back into print in an accessible form, and is convinced of its significance and relevance today. She is Director of the Stirling Smith Art Gallery and Museum, host to the exhibition celebrating the 700th anniversary of the Battle of Stirling Bridge.

Reportage Scotland

Louise Yeoman

ISBN 0 946487 6 8 PBK £9.99

Events, both major and minor, as seen and recorded by Scots throughout history.

Which king was murdered in a sewer?
What was Dr Fian's love magic?
Who was the half-roasted abbot?

Which cardinal was salted and put in a barrel? Why did Lord Kitchener's niece try to blow up Burns's cottage?

The answers can all be found in this eclectic mix covering nearly 2000 years of Scottish history. Historian Louise Yeoman's rummage through the manuscript, book and newspaper archives of the National Library of Scotland has yielded an astonishing range of material, from a letter to the king of the Picts to Mary Queen of Scots' own account of the murder of David Riccio; from the execution of William Wallace to accounts of anti-poll tax actions and the opening of the new Scottish Parliament. The book takes pieces from the original French, Latin, Gaelic and Scots and makes them accessible to the general reader, often for the first time.

The result is compelling reading for anyone interested in the history that has made Scotland what it is today.

Marvellously illuminating and wonderfully readable ANGUS CALDER, SCOTLAND ON SUNDAY

A monumental achievement in drawing together such a rich historical harvest CHRIS HOLME, THE HERALD

Scotlands of the Mind

Angus Calder
ISBN 1 84282 008 7 PBK £9.99

Calder writes like your conscience would THE GUARDIAN

Does Scotland as a 'nation' have any real existence? In Britain, in Europe, in the world? Or are there a multitude of multiform 'Scotlands of the Mind'?

These soul-searching questions are probed in this timely book by prize-winning author and journalist Angus Calder. Informed and intelligent, this new volume presents the author at his thought-provoking best. The absorbing journey through many possible Scotlands – fictionalised, idealised and politicised – is sure to fascinate.

This perceptive and often highly personal writing shows the breathtaking scope of Calder's analytical power. Fact or fiction, individual or international, politics or poetry, statistics or statehood, no subject is taboo in a volume that offers an overview of the vicis-situdes and changing nature of Scottishness. From mythical times to manufactured histories, through Empire and Diaspora, from John Knox to Home Rule and beyond, Calder shatters literary, historical and cultural misconceptions and provides invaluable insights into the Scottish psyche. Offering a fresh understanding of an ever-evolving Scotland, *Scotlands of the Mind* contributes to what Calder himself has called 'the needful getting of a new act together'.

Through the mists beyond our watershed, I hope that what I think I can glimpse might actually emerge – a nation without the disastrous paraphernalia of the nation-state. A nation empowered by acceptance of the realities of its past and ready to generate new Scotlands of the mind, and recreate itself as a land without prejudice. ANGUS CALDER

The Luath Burns Companion

John Cairney
ISBN 1 84282 000 1 PBK £10.00

Robert Burns was born in a thunderstorm and lived his brief life by flashes of lightning
So says John Cairney in his introduction. In those flashes his genius revealed itself.

This collection is not another 'complete works' but a personal selection from 'The Man Who Played Robert Burns'. This is very much John's book. His favourites are reproduced here and he talks about them with an obvious love of the man and his work. His depth of knowledge and understanding has been garnered over forty years of study, writing and performance.

The collection includes sixty poems, songs and other works; and an essay that explores Burns's life and influences, his triumphs and tragedies. This informed introduction provides the reader with an insight into Burns's world.Burns's work has drama, passion, pathos and humour. His careful workmanship is concealed by the spontaneity of his verse. He was always a forward thinking man and remains a writer for the future.

The nearest thing in Scotland to a sex symbol back in the dark days of the White Heather Club THE SCOTSMAN

The trail is expertly, touchingly and amusingly followed THE HERALD (on Cairney's *On the Trail of Robert Burns*)

The Quest For Arthur

Stuart McHardy

ISBN 1 84282 012 5 HBK £16.99

King Arthur of Camelot and the Knights of the Round Table are enduring romantic figures. A national hero for the Bretons, the Welsh and the English alike, Arthur is a potent figure for many. This quest leads to a radical new interpretation of the ancient myth.

Historian, storyteller and folklorist Stuart McHardy believes he has uncovered the origins of this inspirational figure, the true Arthur. He incorporates knowledge of folklore and placename studies with an archaeological understanding of the sixth century.

Combining knowledge of the earliest records and histories of Arthur with an awareness of the importance of oral traditions, this quest leads to the discovery that the enigmatic origins of Arthur lie not in Brittany or England or Wales. Instead they lie in that magic land the ancient Welsh called Y Gogledd, the North; the North of Britain which we now call Scotland.

The Quest For The Celtic Key

Karen Ralls-MacLeod and Ian Robertson

ISBN 0 946487 73 1 HBK £18.99

Who were the Picts? The Druids? The Celtic saints?

Was the famous 'murdered Apprentice' carving at Rosslyn Chapel deliberately altered in the past? If so, why?

Why has Rossslyn Chapel been a worldwide mecca for churchmen, Freemasons, Knights Templar and Rosicrucians?

Why are there so many Scottish connections to King Arthur and Merlin?

What was the famous 'Blue Blanket' of the medieval Guilds of Edinburgh?

Did Prince Henry Sinclair get to North America before Columbus?

The reader who travels with Karen-Ralls MacLeod and Ian Robertson ... will find a travelogue which enriches the mythologies and histories so beautifully told, with many newly wrought connections to places, buildings, stones and other remains which may still be viewed in the landscape and historic monuments of modern Scotland.
REV. DR MICHAEL NORTHCOTT, FACULTY OF DIVINITY, UNIVERSITY OF EDINBURGH

Karen-Ralls MacLeod is endowed with that rare jewel of academia: a sharp and inquisitive mind blessed with a refreshing openness. Her stimulating work has the gift of making the academic accessible, and brings a clear and sound basis to the experiential ... from 'Idylls of the King' to Indiana Jones, the search for the Holy Grail will never be the same again. This is a 'must read' book for all who sense the mystery and magic of our distant past.
ROBERT BAUVAL, bestselling author of THE SECRET CHAMBER and KEEPER OF GENESIS

The Whisky Muse: Scotch Whisky in Poem and Song

Collected and introduced by Robin Laing

Illustrated by Bob Dewar

ISBN 0 946487 95 2 PBK £12.99

Whisky – the water of life, perhaps Scotland's best known contribution to the world

Muse – goddess of creative endeavour

The Whisky Muse – the spark of inspiration to many of Scotland's great poets and songwriters

I first met Robin Laing and Bob Dewar within the hallowed halls of the Scotch Malt Whisky Society in Leith, where Robin and I sit on the Nosing Panel which selects casks of malt whisky for bottling, while Bob executes the famous cartoons which illustrate our findings and embellish the Society's newsletter. The panel's onerous job is made lighter by Robin's ability not only to sniff out elusive scents, but to describe them wittily and accurately, and in this unique collection of ninety-five songs and poems about Scotch whisky he has exercised precisely the same skill of sniffing out treasures. As a highly accomplished singer-songwriter, he also describes them authoritatively, while Bob's illustrations add wit and humour. This splendid book is necessary reading for anyone interested in whisky and song. It encapsulates Scottish folk culture and the very spirit of Scotland. CHARLES MACMEAN, EDITOR, WHISKY MAGAZINE

GENEALOGY

Scottish Roots: a step-by-step guide to tracing your Scottish ancestors
Alwyn James
1 84282 007 9 PB £9.99

HISTORY

A Word for Scotland
Jack Campbell
0 946487 48 0 PB £12.99

Old Scotland New Scotland
Jeff Fallow
0 946487 40 5 PB £6.99

Notes from the North Incorporating a brief history of the Scots and the English
Emma Wood
0 946487 46 4 PB £8.99

ON THE TRAIL OF

On the Trail of Mary Queen of Scots
Keith Cheetham
0 946487 50 2 PB £7.99

On the Trail of Robert Burns
John Cairney
0 946487 51 0 PB £7.99

On the Trail of John Muir
Cherry Good
0 946487 62 6 PB £7.99

On the Trail of Queen Victoria in the Highlands
Ian R Mitchell
0 946487 79 0 PB £7.99

On the Trail of Robert Service
G Wallace Lockhart
0 946487 24 3 PB £7.99

On the Trail of the Pilgrim Fathers
Keith Cheetham
0 946487 83 9 PB £7.99

POLITICS AND CURRENT ISSUES

Scotlands of the Mind
Angus Calder
1 84282 008 7 PB £9.99

Trident on Trial: the case for people's disarmament
Angie Zelter
1 84282 004 4 PB £9.99

Uncomfortably Numb: A Prison Requiem
Maureen Maguire
1 84282 001 X PB £8.99

Scotland: Land & Power – the agenda for land reform
Andy Wightman
0 946487 70 7 PB £5.00

Some Assembly Required: behind the scenes at the rebirth of the Scottish Parliament
David Shepherd
0 946487 84 7 PB £7.99

NATURAL WORLD

The Hydro Boys: pioneers of renewable energy
Emma Wood
1 84282 016 8 HB £16.99

Wild Scotland: the essential guide to finding the best of natural Scotland
James McCarthy
0 946487 37 5 PB £7.50

Wild Lives: Otters – On the Swirl of the Tide
Bridget MacCaskill
0 946487 67 7 PB £9.99

Wild Lives: Foxes – The Blood is Wild
Bridget MacCaskill
0 946487 71 5 PB £9.99

Scotland – Land & People: An Inhabited Solitude
James McCarthy
0 946487 57 X PB £7.99

The Highland Geology Trail
John L Roberts
0 946487 36 7 PB £4.99

'Nothing but Heather!'
Gerry Cambridge
0 946487 49 9 PB £15.00

Red Sky at Night
John Barrington
0 946487 60 X PB £8.99

Listen to the Trees
Don MacCaskill
0 946487 65 0 PB £9.99

ISLANDS

**Easdale, Belnahua Seil, & Luing & Seil:
The Islands that Roofed the World**
Mary Withall
0 946487 76 6 PB £4.99

Rum: Nature's Island
Magnus Magnusson
0 946487 32 4 PB £7.95

LUATH GUIDES TO SCOTLAND

The North West Highlands: Roads to the Isles
Tom Atkinson
0 946487 54 5 PB £4.95

Mull and Iona: Highways and Byways
Peter Macnab
0 946487 58 8 PB £4.95

The Northern Highlands: The Empty Lands
Tom Atkinson
0 946487 55 3 PB £4.95

The West Highlands: The Lonely Lands
Tom Atkinson
0 946487 56 1 PB £4.95

South West Scotland
Tom Atkinson
0 946487 04 9 PB £4.95

TRAVEL AND LEISURE

Die kleine Schottlandfibel [Scotland Guide in German]
Hans-Walter Arends
0 946487 89 8 PB £8.99

Let's Explore Edinburgh Old Town
Anne Bruce English
0 946487 98 7 PB £4.99

Edinburgh's Historic Mile
Duncan Priddle
0 946487 97 9 PB £2.99

Pilgrims in the Rough: St Andrews beyond the 19th hole
Michael Tobert
0 946487 74 X PB £7.99

FOOD AND DRINK

Edinburgh and Leith Pub Guide
Stuart McHardy
0 946487 80 4 PB £4.95

WALK WITH LUATH

Walks in the Cairngorms
Ernest Cross
0 946487 09 X PB £4.95

Short Walks in the Cairngorms
Ernest Cross
0 946487 23 5 PB £4.95

The Joy of Hillwalking
Ralph Storer
0 946487 28 6 PB £7.50

Scotland's Mountains before the Mountaineers
Ian Mitchell
0 946487 39 1 PB £9.99

Mountain Days and Bothy Nights
Dave Brown/Ian Mitchell
0 946487 15 4 PB £7.50

SPORT

Ski & Snowboard Scotland
Hilary Parke
0 946487 35 9 PB £6.99

Over the Top with the Tartan Army
Andy McArthur
0 946487 45 6 PB £7.99

BIOGRAPHY

The Last Lighthouse
Sharma Krauskopf
0 946487 96 0 PB £7.99

Tobermory Teuchter: a first hand account of life on Mull in the early years of the 20th century
Peter Macnab
0 946487 41 3 PB £7.99

Bare Feet and Tackety Boots: a boyhood on the island of Rum
Archie Cameron
0 946487 17 0 PB £7.95

Come Dungeons Dark [Guy Aldred]
John Taylor Caldwell
0 946487 19 7 PB £6.95

SOCIAL HISTORY

Pumpherston: the story of a shale oil village
Sybil Cavanagh
1 84282 011 7 HB £17.99

Pumpherston: the story of a shale oil village
Sybil Cavanagh
1 84282 015 X PB £7.99

Shale Voices
Alistair Findlay
0 946487 78 2 HB £17.99

Shale Voices
Alistair Findlay
0 946487 78 2 PB £10.99

FOLKLORE

Scotland: Myth, Legend & Folklore
Stuart McHardy
0 946487 69 3 PB £7.99

Luath Storyteller: Highland Myths & Legends
George W Macpherson
1 84282 003 6 PB £5.00

Tales of the North Coast
Alan Temperley
0 946487 18 9 PB £8.99

Tall Tales from an Island [Mull]
Peter Macnab
0 94648/ 07 3 PB £8.99

The Supernatural Highlands
Francis Thompson
0 946487 31 6 PB £8.99

MUSIC AND DANCE

Fiddles and Folk
G Wallace Lockhart
0 946487 38 3 PB £7.95

Highland Balls and Village Halls
G Wallace Lockhart
0 946487 12 X PB £6.95

POETRY

Caledonian Cramboclink: verse, broadsheets and in conversation
William Neill
0 946487 53 7 PB £8.99

Men and Beasts: wild men & tame animals
Val Gillies & Rebecca Marr
0 946487 92 8 PB £15.00

Poems to be read aloud
collected and with an introduction by
Stuart McHardy
0 946487 00 6 PB £5.00

Scots Poems to be read aloud
collectit an wi an innin by Stuart McHardy
0 946487 81 2 PB £5.00

CARTOONS

Broomie Law
Cinders McLeod
0 946487 99 5 PB £4.00

FICTION

Milk Treading
Nick Smith
0 946487 75 8 PB £9.99

The Strange Case of RL Stevenson
Richard Woodhead
0 946487 86 3 HB £16.99

But n Ben A-Go-Go
Matthew Fitt
1 84282 014 1 PB £6.99

But n Ben A-Go-Go
Matthew Fitt
0 946487 82 0 HB £10.99

Grave Robbers
Robin Mitchell
0 946487 72 3 PB £7.99

The Bannockburn Years
William Scott
0 946487 34 0 PB £7.95

The Great Melnikov
Hugh Maclachlan
0 946487 42 1 PB £7.95

Luath Press Limited

committed to publishing well written books worth reading

LUATH PRESS takes its name from Robert Burns, whose little collie Luath (*Gael.*, swift or nimble) tripped up Jean Armour at a wedding and gave him the chance to speak to the woman who was to be his wife and the abiding love of his life. Burns called one of *The Twa Dogs* Luath after Cuchullin's hunting dog in *Ossian's Fingal*. Luath Press grew up in the heart of Burns country, and now resides a few steps up the road from Burns' first lodgings in Edinburgh's Royal Mile. Luath offers you distinctive writing with a hint of unexpected pleasures.

Most UK bookshops either carry our books in stock or can order them for you. To order direct from us, please send a £sterling cheque, postal order, international money order or your credit card details (number, address of card holder and expiry date) to us at the address below. Please add post and packing as follows: UK – £1.00 per delivery address; overseas surface mail – £2.50 per delivery address; overseas airmail – £3.50 for the first book to each delivery address, plus £1.00 for each additional book by airmail to the same address. If your order is a gift, we will happily enclose your card or message at no extra charge.

Luath Press Limited
543/2 Castlehill
The Royal Mile
Edinburgh
EH1 2ND
Telephone: 0131 225 4326 (24 hours)
Fax: 0131 225 4324
Email: gavin.macdougall@luath.co.uk
Website: www.luath.co.uk